MW01615149

Through The Fire

Stories of Strength, Courage and Resilience

Presented By
Gwen Goolsby Tillery

ISBN 978-1-5136-9586-0
Printed in USA

Table of Contents

Thank You to Our Sponsors and Supporters

In Loving Memory of Dorothy Goolsby
In Loving Memory of Ottie Taylor
Fred Taylor
Kiersten Tonic
MJ Dear Sis Podcast
In Loving Memory of Mr. Herman West Sr.
In Loving Memory of Mrs. Dorothy May Douglas West
In Loving Memory of Mr. Herman West Jr.
In Loving Memory of Mr. Wendell West
In Loving Memory of Mrs. Charmaine Cynthia Richardson
In Loving Memory of Mrs. Josephine Louise Spivey
In Loving Memory of Mrs. Frances Banks aka Cookie
Mr. Marquise' Khali West Sr.
Mrs. Sarah Evelyn West-Ballard
Mrs. Tierra Cynthia West-Jones & Family
Mrs. Shirley Sanford
Mrs. Diane Cohen-Burton
Ms. D'Javon A. Dupree
Ms. Monique Frazier
Mrs. Wealthy Raynae Blakeney
Mrs. Darla Smith-Threatt
Ms. Tasha Blakeney
Ms. Monique Blakeney
Mrs. Latanya Phillips
Arthur & Jannette Bernard
In Memory of Cecile Stone
Sharon Claiborne
Francine DeLizer-Toombs
Nia Toombs
Michelle Wilson
Global Hand In Hand Properties, LLC
Cheryl Waller-Jackson
SoTA State of the Art Progressive Group
Evelyn Jones
Shantel Patterson

In honor of Hannah and Carlton Lindsay
Kay, Jimmy, Kennedy & Kaylin Lindsay
Victure Hicks & Yasmin Miller
Marquita Devlin
Diva Danielle DeLarge
Andre & Jenelle Sapp Jr.
Brian L. Carter
Aaron Ford
Lena Taylor
Pastor Lois Taylor
In /Memory -Momma Ruth
Clark Godfrey
Benjamin Jeter Jr.
Dominique Francis
Isaiah Peterkin
Latoya Hicks
Derrick & Darlene Jeter
Pastor's Benjamin & Felicia Jeter III
Eric & Ranae Jeter
Cathy Jeter-Shoates
Tyra Hicks
Brian & LaTasha Newkirt
James & Tina Taylor
Eric Overton
Shontina & James Gray
Cherring Spence
Raymond Tyler

Foreword

Gwen and I met by "chance" through the powers of social media when she was looking for a poet for an event they were holding at her and her husband Alex's event venue Picture Perfect Affairs. We got to talking and realized they were supposed to be vendors at my Lyrics to go event that summer. She told me she was interested in having an event similar monthly. My business was brand new, and in an arena, I never thought its direction would go. Needless to say, I was excited and nervous. We had never met, and I wasn't familiar with her place, but somehow, I knew it was meant for me to take this meeting.

I met Gwen and listened to her describe her businesses, specifically Picture Perfect and the 20 years of experience she had in event coordinating leading up to it. After the meeting, I knew I had been led to the person I needed to mentor me in my new business endeavor. Her straightforward, no-nonsense, yet upbeat and caring approach, not just to business but to navigating the inevitable challenges that come, was the guidance I needed to continue The Renaissance Review.

Writing for me is both passion and skill, so I decided to reach back to a business idea I had to offer writing services such as blog/article writing, transcription, editing, and proofreading. I've had a few clients along the way, including a two-year run as a staff writer for Itsthewrightlife.com; however, when she asked me to be one of the editors of this book, I was truly honored to be given the opportunity. When she later asked me to write the foreword, I was humbled.

When she told me more about the book, I knew it was going to be powerful right away. She gathered people from different walks of life to contribute their stories of overcoming anxiety, self-doubt, financial strain, and health scares. Each took a different path, but all were led through and to, the all-powerful God. In each chapter, you will find that faith was the common denominator in their triumphs. That faith propelled them through the fire coming out of the ashes new and whole, knowing who they were, whose they were, and that the power of God lives within them. They overcame the obstacles with that new power and began walking in their purpose.

This book is inspiring, motivating, and empowering. The stories are vulnerable and raw. Through the Fire will resonate with everyone who reads it, no matter what your religion or spiritual practice may be. If you are a believer and facing some of life's most challenging trials and tribulations or if you're seeking to know the power of God for yourself, you've got the right book. It was certainly right on time for me.

Introduction

And they have conquered him by the blood of the Lamb and by the word of their testimony, for they loved not their lives even unto death. This is a brief passage of scripture, but is powerful (Revelation 12:11 ESV). There is deep meaning to these two statements. One statement is built on the work of Jesus and His action. The second statement is built upon the declaration of our testimony to God's work in our lives. We overcome by the word of our testimony, by our faithful commitment to God and by declaring His goodness in our lives. We are even willing to declare that we will not waver from our faith in Him during trials, tribulations or even in the face of death. In this collaboration you get to hear the stories, testimonies of 14 people who felt like at one point in their lives they were in the fire, but just like those three Hebrew boys Shadrach, Meshach, and Abednego (Daniel 3) God allowed us to come through the fire. We are living in times where people have really lost hope and the last 2 years of the pandemic has exacerbated these feelings of hopelessness. It is the hope of the visionary and contributing authors that our stories will offer hope to situations that look hopeless like ours once did. It does not matter what it is, God will see us through if we put our faith and trust in Him. We have come through the fire, we have overcome and we are giving God all the praise.

It is my hope as the visionary that this book would help to encourage, inspire, motivate and even begin to transform how you see yourself and your circumstances. I hope that those feelings of hopelessness will begin to fade and be renewed by these stories of strength, courage and resilience. I want you to know that you too, can come through the fire.

I Am Who God Says I Am

Gwen Goolsby Tillery

It was a surprise when she said, "you struggle with self-doubt". I chuckled and said, "You think I don't". Not only was doubt an issue, but at one point in my life, I feel like everything about me was in question. My complete identity was rooted in fear doubt and feelings of insecurity. How did this happen? More importantly, how did I finally break free of these negative beliefs and become the person who now sees herself as being fearfully and wonderfully made. It has been a long, difficult, and sometimes painful process. The person that I have become is the result of all that I have experienced, endured, encountered, and survived. Not only have I survived, but I've also learned to thrive and now recognize that I was created for a purpose, created to succeed because success is in my DNA.

Let me take you on a journey, of how I have arrived at the place that I am now. The place of understanding that I am Royalty, chosen by God for a specific plan and purpose. It started 52 years ago in a Bronx apartment building with a 2 parent household and 3 older brothers. My upbringing was not chaotic for the most part, but it was filled with some disappointments, heartaches, and pain. This resulted in a distorted view of who I was. It led me to situations and circumstances that were the result of this skewed belief of who I was. What I want you to glean from my story is that all things are possible if you trust God and are willing to do the work to understand who you are and who God is. God will allow all things to work for your good. As I mentioned I did not have a traumatic childhood, but there were definitely some factors that impacted my ability to see the inner beauty, outer beauty, gifts, talents and strengths that were given to me by my mother, father, and most of all my heavenly father. It was not traumatic, but that does not mean there was no trauma.

The early years.... I don't remember much from before the age of 5. One of the most memorable things at the age of 5 is the memory of my Pre-k graduation. I can remember being dressed in my all-white dress, with my white shoes and white graduation cap on. The memory is etched in my mind and so fresh and real as if it just happened. The memory is not of the school, the teacher, or even the ceremony. It was what happened after the graduation that I can remember.

I lived in what is called the projects of the Bronx. Give me a minute to take a bit of a detour here. I promise that I will get back on track. The word project was defined in 2 ways when I looked it up. The first definition and real meaning of the word is an individual or collaborative enterprise that is carefully planned to achieve a particular aim. The second definition, which is used in North America is a government-subsidized housing development with relatively low rents. Let me just take a moment to explore these definitions. The first definition is the original meaning and intent of the word and the second one is what the government decided to call a place where people lived that were from a lower socioeconomic status. So the questions that I have are simply what was the particular aim of the projects, and was the aim or goal achieved? Was I a part of a carefully planned and organized plot by the government? I ask this because we know that the projects of the Bronx and all over America are some of the most crime-ridden, financially challenged, places with some of the lowest levels of education. I am simply asking the question, was this the plan? Was I supposed to fail and become a statistic before I even had a chance to succeed? I can't say for sure that this was the plan, but what I can say is that I am glad that God had other plans for me.

Back to the story... So I had just finished up my little graduation ceremony and I was with my oldest brother Anthony. We were about to head upstairs to our apartment which was on the 17th floor. This wasn't really an issue, except when the elevators were broken and unfortunately this was often in the projects. Well on that day when it was time to head upstairs the elevators were broken. What I remember so fondly from that day was that my big brother picked me up in my little white dress, white shoes, and cap and carried me up the stairs. This would have an impact on me throughout my life. I don't really have many other memories until I get to around the age of 9 to 10.

The pre-adolescent years were not difficult. My mom was always around and I was always around her. I was the youngest of

4 children and the only girl so I spent quite a bit of time around my mother. My dad was always at work or was out, and when he came home he was never really present for many reasons, but the biggest one was that he was often intoxicated as a result of ongoing heavy drinking. By the age of 10, I would say that he had become addicted to alcohol and was definitely an alcoholic. As a result of this, my time and my conversations with him were very limited. Neither of my parents was very affectionate or loving parents, but they were always providers. My parents were hard-working and as a result of this, I never knew struggle and hardship as it related to our finances. Let me be clear, we were by no means rich or even middle class. The bills were paid and there was always food in the refrigerator. I did not want for much and was able to get many of the things that I asked for.

I was never much of a social butterfly, probably because of the insecurities that existed within me. In elementary school, I was not popular, but I was known. My teachers liked me because I was a good student and didn't cause any problems. I was an average student and did not have to work hard in school. One day I was confronted by the Vice-Principal of my middle school. He asked a simple question. Why aren't you on the honor roll? I was in the seventh grade at this time. As I mentioned I was an average student, but I had so much more potential, but so much doubt. That question sparked something in me and challenged me and from that point on I had a different outlook on school. I made the honor roll and by eighth grade, I was inducted into the junior honor society. At my graduation, I received awards and graduated top of my class. I was starting to like school and felt like I mattered, but that quickly changed when I got to High School. The academic rigor and mean girls resulted in me going back into my shell and doubting myself again. I had a few friends, but for the most part, I kept to myself. I did not participate in activities or sports because I was concerned about fitting in. I didn't like drama and the pettiness and this was another reason to keep to myself. Experiencing the ongoing verbal fights between my parents played a big part in me trying to avoid drama. I was bullied in my freshman year, but I managed to make it through without any incidents. By my junior year, I had made a few friends, my grades were back on track, and I started working. My first job was working at a women's clothing store. I enjoyed it and spent much of my pay buying clothes. By my senior year, I had made a few good friends and started working for Jordache in Mid-Manhattan doing data clerking. I didn't really like it, but it allowed me to attend school every other week, which I did love. Although I did well for the most part in school I was not a good test taker. It wasn't that I didn't know the material. I spent so much time doubting myself and not believing myself and as a result, did not do well. I wished that all tests could have been essays because I was always good at writing. So, when it was time to select colleges, I was scared and too intimidated to apply to schools that required the SAT. So I applied to the City University of New York because I knew my GPA and rank would allow me to get in without taking the SAT. I was accepted to Lehman College in the Bronx. I had a better experience in college and made some great friends. These are friends that I still have today. At this point, I was working at a bank and was going to school full time, and maintaining good grades. This should have made me feel good about myself, but it didn't. Despite all the positive things that were going on I was still suffering from low self-esteem and doubt. I still doubted myself and definitely still had problems seeing the beauty that I possessed on the inside and outside. These feelings of inadequacy led to bad decisions when it came to dating, because of how I viewed myself. Let me put out a disclaimer. I did not experience any kind of abuse, but I definitely did not make the best choices.

I graduated from college with my degree in psychology and education and was blessed to start teaching within a few months of graduating. This was the beginning of my career in education. At the age of 22, I was already starting a career and making good money, but my self-esteem was still not intact. By the age of 26, I had Briana, my first daughter, and was finishing up my Masters in Education. It was the birth of Briana that began the process of some deep introspection, as I considered what kind of mother I wanted to be and what kind of life I wanted for my daughter. This is when I began to seek out God and to get a better understanding of who He was. I had Briana dedicated then, at the age of 26 I got saved a few months later. It was her birth that caused me to want to be better and do better and that is exactly what happened. Although I continued to struggle with my self-esteem I started to make better choices so that I would be a role model for my daughter.

I mentioned earlier that I did not have a traumatic childhood, but that there were things that contributed to the skewed perspective I had of myself and that shaped the way I did things or didn't do things. One would think that if you don't come from an abusive background then you should be good, but that is not true. My mother provided me with support and encouragement, but also set high expectations that created in me worry and doubt. She would say things "like don't do things halfway", "If you can't do it 100 percent don't do it". This created a fear of failure that stuck with me for a long time. I didn't want to try something and not be good at it so I didn't try it at all. This was and can still be difficult to overcome. There was always fear and doubt that I or it would not be good enough, even though my life said otherwise. Unfortunately, I was so hard on myself that I did not see the accomplishments. I didn't recognize that I mattered, was worthy of love, and was already enough. I just kept working to prove myself to myself and others. If I just accomplished more and if I just did more then, I would be good. This issue of having to get it right along with the need to please people as a result of the need to please my mother was how I operated for so long. Perhaps I just needed to hear I love you and I and proud of you. I needed to hear it from the person that I tried so hard to please.

Let me be clear I have the heart to give and take care of others, but it came to a point that I was so concerned about everyone else that I had no time to think about myself. This desire to prove myself, to be appreciated for what I could do and not who I was had caused me to lose myself to large extent. Of course, this is what I see now because as they say, "hindsight is 20/20".

Although I had become what most would consider successful based on my achievements, I still was seeking approval and struggling with my identity. Within 6 years of teaching, I was already moving into an administrative role, but again I still had so many doubts about who I was. It's amazing how your childhood experiences can shape so much of your life. Even worse is how it can negatively impact your life if you don't acknowledge and deal with those childhood issues. In retrospect, I realize that many of my decisions and choices were related to who I was as a result of what I had experienced.

Despite this ongoing struggle that took place for many years I am grateful that there was always this desire to become the person God wanted me to be. I also know that despite the shortcomings that my parents may have had, I know with all my heart that they did the best that they could. Not only did they do the best that they could, but they also taught me some great lessons to take with me on this journey called life. My father despite his drinking was a hardworking man and provided for his family until he died and even after that. My mother also taught me the importance of hard work and prayer as well as the importance of having faith. This is interesting because my mother did not attend church when I was growing up, but she taught me biblical principles which have stuck with me. Principles such as hard work, treating people right, being willing to lend a helping hand, being loving towards people, and not being jealous for any reason. Unfortunately, I didn't understand that those attributes were to be applied to my own life. I spent so much of my life trying to be everything to everyone else except myself. I was not able to love myself and value myself the way that I was taught to love and value others.

Here is the good news. This is who I was it is no longer who I am. I have learned to love, value, and appreciate who I am including the flaws while working each day to become better than I was the day before. Better based on God's standard. This can also be your story as well. Sometimes we have to go through the fire to get to where God wants us to be. It's not comfortable but it is necessary.

Let me share with you how I went from always doubting and not loving myself to seeing myself as God sees me. First, let me say that it was not easy. I spent so much of my life measuring myself based on everything and everyone except God. As I said sometimes you will have to go through the fire, but when you come through it you can come out better than when you went in.

So let's fast forward. In 1999 I met my current husband. We moved from NY to NJ in 2000 and got married in 2001. We had our daughter in 2006. Even the pregnancy was one of faith and hard work. During these years I was so focused on my career, and education because I was still proving myself. The girl from the projects still had something to prove. I went back to school to get a second Master's degree, while having a toddler, teenager, husband, and by this time my mother, who was now living with us as a result of dementia. I was completely drained physically, mentally, and emotionally. I was so busy taking care of everything and everyone, but me. I did graduate, but I was exhausted. In the midst of all of this, my husband and I were trying to get a business started and were also very active in the church. I had no time for myself. Or should I say that I made no time for myself. I was not even making time to follow up with routine medical visits. This came at a cost.

In 2012 I had to decide to retire from my career in education as a result of severe herniation and stenosis that I had developed on six levels in my neck. This was huge because the one area of my life that I felt confident and secure in was my career. Having to leave that behind meant I would was losing who I was. My injuries were so significant that I was not able to drive, and had difficulty doing some basic things. The first neurologist that I went to told me that if I didn't have surgery I would be in a wheelchair within 6 months. That I did not accept. It really changed my life and I spent some time grieving who I was, even though I had spent so much energy not appreciating who I was. At the time I felt that I was being punished, but now I know that there is purpose in your pain. This event forced me to begin the process of examining myself and my life once again. It was the beginning of the process of understanding that self-love is not selfish, but it is necessary to become who God has called you to be. Self-love also demands that you do what is necessary to become the best you can be. It forced me to begin the process of healing and growing and recognizing that I was worthy. I began a process of growing closer to God and developing a relationship with God. My desire to please others started to shift to pleasing God. The closer I got to God the more I valued myself and began to recognize how God sees me. I started listening to people like Les Brown for motivation and Joyce Myers to understand the importance of self-reflection on the path to healing. As well as the importance of mindset. Romans 12:2 quickly became one of my go-to scriptures. Do not be conformed to this world, but be transformed by the renewal of your mind, that by testing you may discern what is the will of God, what is good and acceptable and perfect. My thinking, speaking, and actions began to change, and I began to see myself differently. I still had doubts and concerns, but it was different now. Joyce Myers describes the mind as a battlefield, and she is absolutely correct. It became a battle each and every day to keep my mind focused on the word of God and not the works and words of the enemy. Unfortunately at times the enemy was the inner me that continued to operate from a place of fear and worry and not peace and freedom. It is still an ongoing battle, but I am determined to win. My concerns slowly started to shift to pleasing God and making Him happy and not people. I wanted to accomplish what I was created to do. I'm one of those people that literally can have a million ideas in a few minutes so this didn't help me to get clarity as to what it was that God wanted me to do. What was my next assignment? Well, remember that Brother that carried me up the stairs when the elevator was broken. This brother covered me, prayed for me, and help to carry me through once again. His words to me over again were "just do you". What does that mean I asked over and over and would just get the same response? "Just do you". It eventually clicked. It was to become who God created me to be and do what He created me to do. That is what I started to do.

Soon after, I launched my business Spark 2 Inspire, created to help women be equipped spiritually, physically, and financially. In 2020 I rebranded and launched Success Arize, LLC which helps women to become healed, whole and happy so that they can become everything it is that God wants them to be in life, business and ministry. There is a lot that I have left out, but know that the process to get to where I am has taken a lot of work. It required a lot of prayer, tears, and stretching. In this process I lost people that I couldn't cheer for the new me. I stood on one of my favorite scriptures to help me get through, which is Jeremiah 29:11. For I know the plans I have for you, declares the LORD, plans for welfare and not for evil, to give you a future and a hope. This scripture kept me when I wanted to give up when I felt that I wasn't worthy or capable. It was a reminder that God had me.

Understand that life happens in seasons. We are either going into the fire, coming out, or currently in the fire. What you need to know is that God is with you through every stage. God is always refining and trying to get you to the next level and next assignment. In 2017 I decided that I was going to totally surrender to God in all areas of my life. I knew God was calling me to ministry but I did not want to accept the call. Just a few months before my major Women's Conference I developed Bell's palsy. I was devastated. For those that don't know it is a neurological disorder that causes paralysis in your facial muscles. I struggled with speaking, sleeping, and eating. The worse part was the physical appearance of a drooping face and an inability to smile. I felt like it was the worst thing that could have happened and wanted to cancel the conference. It was my commitment to wanting to please God that I continued. This is when I realized that God had done a work in me and that I was no longer the same. I did the conference and began to see myself the way God has always seen me. Despite my inability to smile like I once did, I had a confidence in myself that I had never had before. I truly saw myself as fearfully and wonderfully made by God! This was amazing to me since my outer beauty seemed to be even more flawed and what I thought was my best attribute was now gone.

God had me even when I didn't have myself. He knew that I was royalty, chosen by Him to do the great works that He called me to. My earlier years definitely shaped much of my adult life and it is an ongoing process to ensure that I don't allow those things to continue to impact my life. I still struggle at times to make sure that my life and decisions are not based on the things I experienced as a child, which created the self-doubt and fears. I continue to seek God and speak over my life so that I can experience everything that God has for me. I also practice what I teach so therapy has been a part of this process of becoming healed, whole and happy. I have learned to love myself and take care of myself the way that I once took care of everyone else. Being loving and kind will always be who I am. Now I understand that this does not mean that I sacrifice who God wants me to be. I can value myself and love myself the way that God does so that I can fulfill what He has for me. I want to leave you with these scriptures. I hold them dear to my heart because they help me to stay in the place that God wants me to be in. They remind me who I am, and what I've been created to do.

Therefore, if anyone is in Christ, he is a new creation. The old has passed away; behold, the new has come 2 Cor 5:17 ESV. This keeps at the forefront of my mind that who I once was is no longer who I am. I have been renewed by the blood of Jesus. 1 Peter 2:9 But you are a chosen people, a royal priesthood, a holy nation, God's special possession, that you may declare the praises of him who called you out of darkness into his wonderful light. This is a powerful reminder of so many things. I am reminded that I have been chosen by God, that I am ROYALTY and that I have been called out of darkness into light. This light is not about me, but it is for others to see so that they may inquire about who this Jesus is. For God hath not given us the spirit of fear, but of power, and of love, and of a sound mind 2 Tim 1:7. I remind myself that if it is fear it is not God. It also reminds me that as I continue on this journey it should be done in love and that my mind must be rooted in who God is. I have to remember that I am who God says I am.

THROW THE FISH BACK IN

Mrs. Gwendolyn M. West-Sutton

This story is an excerpt from the soon to be published book entitled "Throw The Fish Back In!"

Having been baptized by fire and surviving the unfortunate experience of Teenage Dating Violence, I want to thank God for being with me, while I was in the fire and being with me, as He brought me through the fire. I am eternally grateful to God that something positive eventually came out of my suffering. Moreover, I am exceedingly grateful to God for sparing the lives of my family members, after I had put them at risk; the result of my foolish behavior and bad choices. More specifically, my Mother, my Father, my Sister and my Brother. In addition, I thank God for sparing my life. What I didn't know is that God was using that experience, the experience of Teenage Dating Violence, to give birth to a child, a concept and a conference. What I know now is that I had too much free time during the summer. I should have been involved in some structured activities, dance class, gymnastics, something. I also know that if God intended for me to have that experience for the greater good, no matter how many structured activities I was involved in, it would not have made a difference. I got my PHD (Prayer Heals Devastation) from attending the "School of Hard Knocks" and was baptized by fire in the process. As I was attending this school, I was not always apt to listen to or obey my parents and was engaging in activities that were not age appropriate. Sadly, I started to engage in the dating game before I knew anything about the game of life and before I developed a life plan, to prepare for my future.

You see, I was a girl who had her first official boyfriend at the age of twelve, too early, too soon and with no skills. That boyfriend kicked me to the curb at the age of fourteen. I was devastated! I was tore up from the floor up! I was an emotional mess! My self-esteem was lowered to the point that I was willing to accept anyone, anyone, in my life who would have me. When I met Mr. A (I'm using a pseudonym to protect the not innocent at all!), he was sixteen and I was fifteen. Too early, too soon and with no skills. He chose me and then things got worse in my life. You see, I was still vulnerable and tore up from the prior breakup. He told me what I could expect. He told me what he was capable of doing to me. He actually told me that he had hit and was violent with his previous girlfriend. Who knows he could have been dating us both at the same time. Sadly, for some strange reason, silly me, I thought it was her fault. Maybe I wasn't really listening to what it was he was actually saying. I was probably too busy talking and blinded by the cuteness or trying to show how worthy I was to be his girlfriend.

In a very short time after that he started to abuse me emotionally and physically. Horrifyingly, one night after we had gone to see a movie, I thought he was going to walk me home, but he decided that he wanted us to go to his house instead. I didn't want to go. So, all I said was, "No." As we were walking down the street all of a sudden, he slapped me in my face so hard I got cut from my eye down to my chin. This happened in public! There were people outside! I'll never forget hearing a man say, "Hey man, don't be hitting her like that. Take her home and do that." Well, my thoughts were gee thanks mister, I think. I guess he thought he was being funny. But, if it had happened to his mother, sister or daughter, his attitude more than likely would have been different. Meanwhile, back to and after the slap, you would have thought I would have thrown that Fish, Mr. A back in! Unfortunately, and sadly I did not!

You would think that after I had that awful experience that I would have learned some thangs and moved on. Also, you would probably think I was a glutton for punishment. Looking back at that period of time, it seemed like I was. But you don't understand; he apologized, said it would never happen again. According to him nobody else loved him but me, and so on. So, I learned we must be ready and alert when playing the Dating Game because if we are not, there's a great possibility that we could find ourselves in an abusive relationship or have our hearts broken again and again. It's sad to say that many of our potential intimate dating partners do not deserve to occupy space in our lives. That's why it's important for us to be on a fact-finding mission. We must close our mouths and really listen to what they are telling us about themselves.

Remember Mr. A? The one who told me everything that he was going to do to me or the things that he was capable of doing to me? One summer day after I had gotten paid from my summer job, my coworker and I went shopping well into the evening. As soon as I had gotten off the bus, after returning home, several of my neighbors approached me stating that Mr. A was looking for me. Before I could get to my house, there he was questioning me like we were grown, married or he owned me. After being in his presence for a few minutes I went into the house and my mother asked me, "What was wrong?" Of course, I said nothing, knowing all the time I was scared. He then called me on the telephone asking me to meet him at 16th and Berks Streets. Like a fool I did. As soon as he saw me he gripped me up under my arm and forced me to go to his house. He then directed me to lie across his bed and began to hit me with something that was like a paddle on my buttocks. Fortunately for me and unfortunately for him there was a knife on a small table in the room. Yes, you guessed it, I grabbed that knife and he tried to take it from me and he cut his hand. When he went into the kitchen to get something to stop the bleeding, I ran out of that house as fast as my short legs could carry me and went into a neighborhood store where my friend worked. She locked the door and I called my parents. My dad, Herman Sr. and everybody who lived on the street that I lived (well it seemed like everybody), came to get me. Some of them may have been genuinely concerned and others to be nosey. Of course, my oldest brother, Herman Jr. would have been with my dad if he wasn't stationed in Biloxi, Mississippi serving in the U.S. Air force. You see, if I had closed my mouth and actually listened, I would have really heard what that Fish, Mr. A, previously said to me and should have known what to expect. Moreover, I would have known that Fish was not for me. Remember, he told me he was violent with another girl he had dated. You would think that after the abuse I later experienced, I would have thrown that Fish back in. Foolishly, I did not!

One summer day Mr. A brought somebody's jacket to my house and left it there. Later that evening, I became aware of the fact that he was at a house party on the next block from the street I lived on. It was the kind of home where the parents oftentimes were not there because they were somewhere engaging in their party activities. So, that house was a place where young people hung out and did whatever they wanted to do. I was irritated because he should have taken the jacket that he left at my house with him. Somehow, I became emboldened and decided that I was going to take that jacket to him at the party house. I know, you're probably wondering, what was I thinking! Clearly, I wasn't thinking. I knocked on the door, asked to speak to him, gave him the jacket, and left. What I didn't know at first was that he left too! I realized that he was following me as I was walking down the street. My heart began to race because I was scared and I tried to walk faster than my short legs were able to carry me. He then caught up with me and started saying some things to me. I didn't remember any of it. All I know is that we were outside and I didn't want to be embarrassed!

All of a sudden, he grabbed hold of me by my blouse and, (since this was happening in public and evidently, I had a burst of courage), I grabbed hold of him by his shirt. I thank God that He sent me an angel. Some guy that lived in the neighborhood came and separated us. I then wanted to run down the street into the next block where I lived, but my pride would not let me. So, I walked as fast as my short legs would allow. Then God sent me another angel, a defending and protecting angel, my brother Wendell who just happened to be standing outside the apartment building where we lived. Mr. A approached me and wanted to talk to me to which I told him, "I didn't want to talk." He persisted in his attempt to talk to me and my brother told him that I didn't want to talk. My brother then said, "Come on Gwen." He and I began to walk across the street and then down Euclid Street. Mr. A began to follow us, continuing his attempt to talk to me. My brother then said, "She said she didn't want to talk." However, Mr. A persisted. All of a sudden, my brother turned around and started hitting and punching Mr. A. To my surprise and amazement, he did not fight my brother back! The reason I was so amazed is because Mr. A had no problem hitting me. Later that evening Mr. A was calling my house and leaving threatening messages. So, my brother and I planned to accompany each other wherever we ventured to go over the next several days. However, what I didn't know or expect, but probably should have, was that we would see him the very next day. When my brother and I saw him on 17th Street near Cecil B. Moore Avenue, my heart almost stopped! What I didn't expect was for him to be cordial and civil. Furthermore, I was not expecting to see the effects from the one-sided fight. He had a black eye and other scars as the result of the altercation that he had with my brother. Once again, he was apologetic to me. Surely, you would have thought that I would have thrown that Fish back in. Yes, you've guessed it, I did not!

Even though I had been experiencing teenage dating violence as a youth, I did not know what to call it. For a long time, I was not even aware that there was a cycle to it. I didn't share with my parents nor my siblings what I was going through. That was another bad choice and a major mistake because, if I had informed them, I would not have had to suffer in that deep, dark, scary place in my life for as long as I did. I would not have had to suffer in silence and be alone. Moreover, like many people who were or are in similar situations, I protected the abuser by lying, covering up, or making excuses for my visible emotional distress, as well as any visible scars. What's even more absurd is he had a tendency to make me feel sorry for him and acted as if I was the only person who loved and cared about him. In addition, after each traumatic episode, he was extremely apologetic, even remorseful and claimed, of course, that it would never happen again. Unfortunately, I fell for the okie doke again and again!

Sadly, I continued in the relationship evidently as the result of having low self-esteem; I cared more about him, more than I cared about myself. In addition, I wasn't thinking about my future, my life or the possible hardships that remaining in that relationship could or would prevail. You see, I was a girl who was in the twelfth grade trying to decide what I was going to do when I graduated from high school. Now, how sad was that? The reason why I say it was sad is because I should have known in elementary school what I was going to do when I graduated from high school. At the very least, I should have known that I was going to attend college. I should have had a life plan. Unfortunately, the situation was even more critical. You see, I was pregnant by an abusive person who didn't have a life plan of his own. Eventually, I was left all alone to endure the pregnancy and the consequences of being a teenage single mother. One day, when I was on my way to school minding my own business going to get my education (even though I didn't know what I was going to do with it, I kept going to get it), he approached me and said, "Give me a dollar." I said, "I didn't have it.", but he knew my parents had given me lunch money. All of a sudden, he drew his fist back and punched me in my face so hard he blacked my eye! Needless to say, I had to endure going to school and walking around with that embarrassing black eye for at least a week, if not more, and having to endure people asking me the question. "What happened to you?" Even though, many of them already had heard something about what had happened through the grapevine. Back then we heard things through the grapevine. Thank God it didn't happen in this day and age because it may have been posted on Facebook, Instagram, tweeted on Twitter or seen on some other social media site and shared at least a million times! Thank God for small favors!

Unfortunately, a Bad Boy chose me to be his girlfriend and I blindly accepted. But, let me tell you, I had a Badder Momma, Dorothy was her name and sister, Sarah! You see my Momma, my sister, and one of my momma's best-friends; her butcher's knife went looking for him. My family didn't play that! They were not going to allow anyone to hurt me if they could help it. (Oh and of course, it happened over 40 years ago. It's definitely not safe to go looking for an abuser nowadays because the abuser may shoot you, your Momma and the entire family.) When I got home from school that day, my sister said, "Girl when we saw him, I cornered him and Momma slapped the s**t out of him, pointed her butcher's knife in his face and said, "Mother F****r", if you ever put your Mother F*****g hands on my daughter again I will cut you too short to s**t!". I didn't know my Momma was gangster! To keep it moving, finally, the light came on from that blue light special and I'm not talking about from K-Mart; I'm talking about from that punch in the eye...That Fish, that boyfriend, was not for me. Sadly, too many of us know what I'm talking about. We know what that blue light special looks and feels like. That's why I don't understand it when I hear some females say they want a Bad Boy. My question is, why? Trust me, it's not a good choice. I've been there, done that and got the black-eye amongst other things to prove it. Not intentionally of course. I didn't know how to play the Dating Game. I just wasn't paying attention to the warning signs; one of Lady-G's (that would be me), Rules for Engagement in the Dating Game.

At this point, all I can say is Hallelujah, thank you Jesus! I don't remember exactly when it happened or exactly how it happened. All I know is that by God's grace and mercy, it did! I was blessed that God brought an end to that dark, scary, incredibly sad time in my life. However, as crazy as this may sound, I am grateful for that experience now that I am out of that situation of course; because God gave me a message out of my mess!

After having been baptized by fire, by God's grace and mercy I survived the horrible experience of Teenage Dating Violence and I came forth as pure as gold. Let me explain, while I know that I am a flawed spiritual being having a human experience, I understand that I have been refined by going through the fire of experiencing Teenage Dating Violence. Moreover, I know that God used His creative nature in me to manifest something for the greater good. I was blessed with a message out of my mess! He blessed me to give birth to the concept of "Throw The Fish Back In". In addition to a ministry that is focused on empowering women.

As I reflect on that sad and unfortunate time in my life, I know that it was only by GOD's grace and mercy that I survived and was able to be set free from that horrific experience. He blessed me with His presence, a loving family, and a community village that provided me with the support I needed, even when I was not aware that I needed their assistance. Just as importantly, God blessed me with the spirit of forgiveness. With respect to my community village, He provided me with a Ms. J., who happened to be looking out of the window that day and witnessed the punch in my face that resulted in me having a black eye. She could have thought that it was none of her business and could have done nothing. Instead, as God would have it, she called my mother on the phone and alerted her to what had just transpired. With respect to my family, God blessed me to have my sister walk with me to school that day, after I was assaulted. Yes, I still had to go to school that day. Moreover, He filled my mother and my sister with the necessary passion needed to pursue my abuser and helped them find that Fish, to confront him on my behalf. In addition, it was some people that lived on the street that I lived on that accompanied my father when he came to get me after I had the awful experience with that incident with the paddle and the knife. Once again I covered for Mr. A so my dad didn't know what was happening.

It was God's amazing grace that awakened me to the fact that love doesn't hurt, I needed to put myself first and have some rules for engaging in the Dating Game. Moreover, it wasn't my responsibility to be more concerned about the abuser, than I was about myself, risking my life and well-being. As I was blessed with these new revelations, I had an epiphany that God used to bless my soul and saved my life. I became enlightened to the fact that I deserve better and I needed to love myself, before even considering loving someone else. Moreover, I needed to be more selective about who I allowed to have a front-row seat in my life. In addition, I needed to use the dating process as a fact-finding mission and close my mouth and listen. I learned that it was more important for me to be an active listener, as opposed to a constant speaker. The realization that it was more important for me to really hear what these potential mates were saying and what they were not saying; was paramount to preventing myself from getting involved in abusive relationships, in the future. Furthermore, I learned that any and every male is not worthy of being in my life and especially not in my bed. Consequently, I no longer felt the need to share information about myself, when I was on a date, as if I was a female thirsty for love, in essence saying, "Pick me, pick me!" More importantly, I learned that making the wrong decision about who I allow in my life, could possibly cause me to lose my life.

The writing of my story was a very interesting process. It required me to dig deep down into the recesses of my mind and memory bank, to go back to a very dark place and sad time in my life. Although the abusive relationship spanned about four years, I received an education that would last me a lifetime. Again, it was the presence of God in my life that opened the way to allow for the intervention and support I received from my family and community village. In addition, it was the blessing of the spirit of forgiveness that set me free from the negative energy that would have kept me connected to that experience and the abuser. It's a blessing that I was able to forgive that Fish and set us both free from that traumatic time in our lives. I am eternally grateful to God for blessing me with a forgiving spirit; because, if I had not been able to forgive my abuser, I would not have been able to love my husband wholly and completely.

It is my belief that as we make our journey through this life, we will have a variety of experiences that will run the gamut. Oftentimes, they will involve issues with relationships with our intimate dating partners, you know, our boos, our mates, or whatever you choose to call him or her. Too frequently, the issues in our relationships can become fiery, inflamed and explode into a full-fledged fire. I believe it is extremely important to have an intimate relationship with God, a daily spiritual practice, a fire extinguisher, so to speak, an ever-present help, to undergird us when the flames of life are out of control. For those of you who are in the fire, you should be encouraged, for God is with you, even if you don't feel His presence. For those of you who have not yet gone through a fire, know that God will be with you, as well, again even if you don't feel His presence. Finally, and more importantly, know that like I, God will be with you and will bless you too, as He allows you to survive, as He grows you too, through the fire.

The Voice

Pastor Anthony E. Goolsby

As I look back on my life I can see key days, great days, and powerful days. Days that decisions were made or not made that had great consequences. I am glad that I am writing this because sometimes we tend to mentally negate the power of a day.

Time will not allow me to go back to the very beginning, but this may be a good starting point on this day in NYC, I can see myself running down the street in the light of day with a shotgun, a bag of money, and a bag of tokens it was about a quarter-mile run from the train station we had robbed on Bay Ave to where I lived and where we changed clothes and stashed the tokens till things cooled down. As soon as I walked into the house my Mother asked what was going on. Wow, young people never underestimate a mother's sixth sense. Of course we said nothing as we could hear police sirens screaming up and down our block. Looking out the window we saw a plain clothes man combing the block.

I remember thinking all this for a couple of hundred bucks and two bags of tokens. Well, we got away with that and I remember thinking what if I had to pop that guy in the token booth? What if someone had gotten in our way, they would have to die for a couple of bucks and two bags of tokens. I could have ended up in jail for a few bucks and two bags of tokens. Today I know it was God's grace that none of that happened because we pulled that job with the finesse and skill of the apple dumpling gang.

Yeah that was a big day as I sit here with tears in my eyes thanking God for grace and mercy. Because of that day I saw where my life was heading. I saw Rikers Island as clear as day when I was not built for that, so that day I decided to take my Army commitment seriously. Thank you Grandma for praying. I left for the Army on the appointed day, but let me tell you something that moment of clarity I had was gone quickly, and it was my plan not go. My Grandmother had come up from South maybe to see me off, or maybe just following the guidance of the Holy Spirit but she was there and she was happy I was going in the Army. The entire time I am thinking about how I am going to pull this off without breaking her heart. Maybe God knew she was the only person that I had that kind of love for, that I would honor her feelings and keep my word. So I left for Fort Jackson, South Carolina

The Army was fairly easy for me. I was in great shape from B ball and running up and down the 17 floors to my apartment back in the Bronx. I loved guns, bombs and fighting so I should have excelled, but I just had this greater love for drugs alcohol and stealing.

There were some hard times but I made it. I remember the day orders (assignments) got passed out, that was the day of my assignment to Germany. I was heartbroken. I wanted to go to Korea. 95 % of people went to Korea for their assignment. There were lots of things you could do to get your assignment changed to a very easy task, but not for me I tried everything with no luck.

But one thing I know for sure is if you were a couple of days late coming back from leave they would cut you a new assignment. So I came back two weeks later, ha-ha got you. So I wake up the next morning thinking I am going to the administration office for a new assignment, God you got jokes. I am on the bus going to the airport for my old assignment. Yep God you got jokes. Korea is totally off the table guess there will be no major drug trafficking and human trafficking in my immediate future. So here I am in Germany. Oh my my, was I wrong about Germany. Germany in the '70s to early 80s was heaven there were drugs and women everywhere I mean drugs in an abundance and availability even greater than New York. So I am having a blast not doing well in the army but having a total blast.

Of Course, my career is not going well, but by this time I have also found a wonderful woman. I don't mean to mention her like an afterthought but, if I were to start to tell you about her it would pull me in directions that would not serve the purpose of this writing. Just so you know I am still married to her after taking her for a walk of hell and hard knocks. The day I met her was also a day because while in the deepest saddest part of my addiction she held it together so when I was ready I had something to recover for. Thank you baby. Sorry I have not always paid you back as I should have but, I am not done yet.

So my Army career lasted all of 10 years and I believe my claim to fame is how I took underachieving to new heights without getting dishonorably discharged. Now I am a civilian and free of the Army, as always with big dreams and that which I have always been told. I have always been told that I had unlimited potential. At this point, addiction gets really hard but I'm a hustler from New York. I can make it work but it's not working. Things are falling apart. It's not like when I was in the Army where I could just go get help. Not like it worked then, but now I really need help. Then came a day it was like the scales fell from my eyes things began to add up and the sum was a bit too much. I needed help so I surrendered my Pride and got the help I needed. This is where the story starts that I want to share with you. I got clean and sober. I took to a new lifestyle, spent tons of time with my sober brothers and sisters, took the steps that they suggested, and met with them often to share experiences, strength, and hope. Life was becoming really good. I was actually living a good life. No more drugs and alcohol. I started to pursue new things and my family life was much improved. I rediscovered my long-lost love of sports. I started playing B-ball with the local teenagers and it didn't take me long to get my touch back. I was traveling around the city kicking butt and taking names along with that. I had developed a passion for bodybuilding and soon went hardcore. So after a hard day of working on a moving truck anywhere from 8-12 hours, I would then head to the gym or the B-ball court in the spring or summer. You could imagine I was in very good shape. The B-ball crew had always been asking me to club with them but I always said no, but at some point, it was someone's birthday and I went. I remember it just like it was yesterday. MC Hammer Pumps and a Bump was playing loud and the bass was thumping. The dance floor was empty but I walked in the club, walked directly to the dance floor and hit it like it was my mine. In 2 minutes I was dancing with two young ladies and I was hooked, not to the girls but the thrill of being that guy. My guys joined in and soon the floor was packed but we were the center of attention. Just like that on to a new addiction. You see it wasn't drugs or drinking, but it was a reality bender something to fill that big hole in my gut. So I found myself hooked on clubbing and I had to get more muscle, more muscle, more muscle so I could hide who I really was, a scared little boy who was afraid you would see him, approach him and he might cry or run away. With all this muscle I was armored up just like when I was high I was relaxed and unafraid of you. That feeling that I get does not make me feel superior, but equal. I remember the first time I drank, I can still remember that feeling of just being one of the guys. I also remember telling myself this is something I have to do more of. Well, I have found my new drink and drug. Hardcore bodybuilding and nightlife. Man, my ego was out of control, my real afraid self was hidden under pounds of muscle and pride in my reputation in the city. To make it even worse, I then discovered flirting the ultimate proof that you're somebody I became very good at it. That's my problem getting good at things that feed my ego. So everywhere in every situation, I had to speak to women, make them smile, and make them show interest in me. My greatest thrill was being in the city on a warm Saturday afternoon and being recognized and greeted every few minutes. Ego fed.

It was pretty disgusting and to be pitied. So to my lovely wife, I said and still say sorry after years of addiction. Now you're stuck with a grown man who is acting like the spoiled high school quarterback. I was actually away from home more than when I was using drugs and alcohol. Sometimes I clubbed from Thursday to Saturday. In all this I thought I was fine. The jobs started getting better and money was no longer a problem. I was a mile wide and an inch deep, simply shallow. I was sad and hurt inside. The good thing about drug addiction is you know what your problem is. At this point I didn't know what my problem was. I knew deep inside, if and when I would look something would be missing. What could it be, things were better than ever? Everything looked great. My relationship with my wife looked great but I could tell she wasn't happy, why we were rocking out gifts and vacations. Your husband was a well-known guy around town. Truth is I did wonder why she wasn't really happy, but was always afraid to ask. I could tell, and I knew that my daughter needed more from me even if she didn't. Unfortunately, in the world we live in if you have a Black American father and he stayed with you that's like a claim to fame in itself. I have actually been told by other Black European girls in our city that they hated my daughter when they were young because she had a father in the house, well I was there in the physical but again my ego and my unhealed self was hidden under superficial BS and that little boy that was really afraid who really didn't know how to show love. I was dominated by ego and had found a way to feed it and that let me feel sort of ok just like the Heroine did. I might have felt alright but an important job went undone. I am sorry baby I am not finished making it up to you.

That's a glimpse into my early life and forgive me, if I repeat myself everything seemed good but I was still empty inside just like when I was using H and actually I was still using just not H. Damn things looked good. The wife and I had started taking vacations tasting the finer things in life. You see, my wife had a well-paying job and my emptiness led me to seek even satisfaction via my job so it was nothing for me to do a 16 hour day so money was ok. I loved vacations. Let me tell you something there is something about being buffed and a black American in these European vacation spots so my ego was in full bloom and I loved it. Greece was my favorite. Like I already mentioned I really didn't have a need to have actual relationships outside my marriage but I needed the attention and man did I enjoy it on those vacations. Wow, again I ask is it possible that I could ever make up for that behavior with my wife. I don't think so but by the power of Jesus Christ, I am going to keep trying.

One year we decided that we would go to Cyprus. I thought it would be like Greece and for political reasons Americans were not supposed to travel there. Well my Ego loved the idea of saying I have been somewhere that the average American has not been and technically couldn't go. What a great life!!!!. Then why do you feel so empty? I had a kind of you're there feeling but could not figure out exactly where there was. So off to Cyprus and oh my, what a disappointment at least upon early arrival.

The things that stroked my ego caused me not to do proper research on the Island of Cyprus. In 1960 Cyprus became independent of Britain (it had been a crown colony since 1925) as the Republic of Cyprus. But the English influence was still super strong and that's not what I wanted in a vacation. Added to that, the prices were insane and the food was at best ok. The hotel was the worst it was rated 5 stars but compared to what we were accustomed to it was a 3 at best but different places different standards. The very worst and mean the worst was there was a group of people there in large numbers whose culture, traditions, and way of vacation were in my opinion was totally disgusting.

I am sorry and I thought long and hard before I wrote that but that is my truth they were often drunk, loud, and had the table manners of a wild boar. Bear with me we are going somewhere with all this. On top of all this the beaches were ugly and gravel filled. I hated that because my wife really like the beach and that was her enjoyment, me being melanated I was not found lying in the sun. So our first day there was such a disappointment. The next day also, but we had met another couple so it was a bit better. Then the third night came, I heard music and thought I should investigate it. What a party I had stumbled upon. I mean a party with people dancing all along the bar and on tables. I was in my world. It doesn't take long for me to meet the right people. I met some adult magazine publishers that traveled with an entourage and all the right party favors, Now I was not using drugs anymore and had no desire to cheat on my wife, but that just made it even better for my main problem, my Ego. I was partying and being the center of attention, the life of the party and did not need drugs. I would be in the club and attracted so much attention because of the arrogant attitude I had. I was so self- assured that it seem to create even more interest from the women in the clubs. I had the hottest woman flirting with me and I had no intention of really reciprocating. I was surprised I could even get out on the door. My ego was so inflated I was literally drunk. I was the man pumped up off the most powerful drug there is pride, ego and self-worship. I partied till about 8 in the morning. Went back to the wife I had neglected. Took a 2-3 hour nap and then tried to make a nice day with her needless to say the day wasn't very good for either of us the Island was really nothing special, the hotel was mediocre at best. But I don't want to bore you so I will say that's basically how the next few days went. We took a few bus tours and all I did was sleep on the bus and at the destination, I was like a friendly zombie. I know my wife was having a terrible time, but I was so powerless over that nightlife I would tell myself tonight I was staying in but never did or never could. I loved my wife then and just like I love her now. I had to do something. I think it was in the Lobby of the hotel that I saw an advertisement for a 3 stop cruise and on the advertisement board, it showed people dressed in semi-formal evening wear at dinner. That's it I will book that cruise and then I can't party because there would be no party at least not the kind I needed. So there we were on a boat stuck with these dead no life having folks doing the semi-formal evening thing. I hope I was somewhat able to hide from my lovely how much I disliked this but my hope was she liked it. First, stop Lebanon a very interesting place not much to look at but the history and the people made wish we could spend a few days there, Next stop Egypt the pyramids and the Sphinx in my opinion highly overrated just looked like some old stuff to me but Cairo was very interesting the population density blew my mind along with the museum.

My last and final stop was Israel a place I had always wanted to see and know a little about. I was not Christian but I was familiar with it from my youth. So not only was it a place I really wanted to see and I understood the magnitude of its history, it was also the last stop. In two more days, I would be back on Cyprus. As interesting as it was, I didn't feel good because I was not getting the opportunity to feed this new addiction of having my ego fed. So off we went seeing a lot of very interesting things and our last stop was The Church of the Holy Sepulcher. So I am checking everything out being grateful that I, a recovering junkie born in Harlem raised in the Bronx, could get to see this.

At that point, I remember looking over at the slab that Jesus had rested on after his crucifixion. You know the one that they found no one on that third day. There was this guy kneeling at it crying and he was rubbing crosses on it. I had no idea at the time what he was doing and why he was crying I made some sort of derogatory comment in my mind. That is when I heard a voice call me, I looked but didn't see anyone. Then I heard it again and still didn't see anyone. Strangely I thought I am buggin and now the third time I hear the voice it seems to come with more power. I hear it in a place that I have never heard anything before somewhere deep in me. I start to weep really weep me the G, the coolest of the cool. I really start to weep and sob like a baby and its beautiful and I know it is Jesus I just know it. I know at this point that I have to decide yes or no. I began to say yes, yes, yes or actually crying yes, yes. Now folks are looking at me. I am sure my wife is thinking this fool has relapsed and he is on some type of drug. I noticed the tour guide had this knowing look on his face like he had seen this before. People were looking but no one intervened or interrupted. I said yes to Jesus I felt different from that day on, notice I said I felt different I didn't say I did differently. We got back to the Island and I went back to the clubs. They didn't seem the same. I still loved to dance but something was different. I think I even started back to the room before daylight.

Well, it's time to come home now and I had no idea what to do. I know I said yes to Jesus but I actually had no idea what that was supposed to look like. My wife had a friend who was a Christian to whom I told my story and she said we should look for a church, so we did. It took at least four weeks visiting here and there. Sometimes I knew as soon as I walked in the place and sometimes it took a little while but by the end of service I knew this was not it.

New Life Christian Fellowship with its wonderful loving and wise Pastors is where it started. I knew it was the place for me by the Spirit and nothing else. I just knew it, by the same means that I know the others were not. I knew 100% this was it. I was too Christian dumb to have an agenda, to Christian dumb to know that it was one of those crazy word of faith type places, tongue talking, faith healing, tithe paying places I only know that the same voice that I said yes to said yes to this place. I will share one thing with you that made this place so special. Yep, it was a bit charismatic and very strict but they had love and wisdom. It was the example of the love and wisdom I encountered there. I had been coming for maybe 4-5 weeks now and my wife didn't seem interested. I asked the First Lady How I could make her come to church. She told me you can't make her come but try this, lovingly invite her. Every time you come to church return home happier, nicer and sweeter than you left. Let her see the change in your life just grow as a husband. It was the wisdom of the place that the voice led me to.

The reality is I was chasing Christ, but I was still clubbing, I would come to Bible study on Wednesday and after that go to the Club for urban and hip hop night and they knew this in church, but they just kept loving on me and feeding me the word. No one said anything. So when the time was right I was told that my club days should be over, but told by the right person at the right time. Let me tell you about it a big-time DJ is coming down from Berlin. I am coming from Bible Study so I am there a bit early. I am standing around waiting on my crew to show up and I hear this voice say Son that's enough. I think in my head excuse me, and I hear it again "that's enough". I knew who it was and I knew what He meant. I have not been in that type of club again. That was 1999. Here is the point my job is to love you and teach you it's up to the Holy Spirit to change you. Stop telling people what they need to do if they are sitting under good teaching and they are being prayed for the Holy Spirit will speak or move at the right time.

When you are having issues or problems do the best you can on a daily basis God knows how to heal his people. You have to know how to allow him to heal you.

Stop wondering how and when you are going to overcome, don't give up, have faith, keep on keeping on keep your ears and your heart open, God will move. It is the job of the Holy Spirit to lead us to change. Avoid those who judge and seek those who encourage.

At this point I have grown by leaps and great bounds under the love, prayers, and teaching of this Ministry. Man look where I have come from and a few short years later where I am holding positions in the church as a servant and trusted leader. This is it. Fast forward our Pastors must leave. Man, I am afraid. But the voice assures me it is better for me if they leave. So I stumble around a bit not really finding where I should be not long but too long. So I am visiting a church I have visited a few times before, not because I like it but because I was taught that I should be in church on Sunday. I still believe that I have no intention of staying here. It was to quote me, really raggedy. I go to the bathroom, my mind full of negativity about this place. And then it happens again and I know 100% what it said "Son you are my chosen Vessel in this place" I can't tell you how unhappy I was with the Voice, but I know better than to follow my voice. I had a whole life time of emptiness following my voice.

So here I am at what I will call church two. The names must be changed as it is not my intention to place blame or cause offense. So I heeded the voice, and I learned being His chosen vessel could be hard work. I was there to expose and rebuke which is hard enough, but when the leader does not see what you see and he is better friends with those who wish to use him than he is with you, it made the assignment extremely difficult. My first fruits were hurt and frustration with a dash of embarrassment. I was actually rebuked for trying to hold people accountable, and for attempting to follow God's direction. What made it worse was that the rebuke came from the person I was trying to protect. Then came a written rebuke. It was a very painful time, but what could I do? I am following the voice. I followed the voice and it took a while and soon those who were not in order were stripped of their unofficial power. In spite of my hurt feelings I kept my trust in the voice and these people were exposed and with many witnesses. The voice literally led me to the right place at the right time. Pastor and I began to get along really well and we became a powerful one-two punch for the Lord and his people I can't tell you how much I learned about healing and deliverance during this time and not to mention the power of brotherhood. He and I traveled as far as Latvia teaching and preaching freedom to the saints. We studied together, laughed together, cried together and forgave each other of many mistakes but the evil one came in and planted seeds and he used circumstances to his advantage. Throw in a Jezebel and our relationship was done for. Things began to happen that were just downright disrespectful. This is when the voice began to tell me it was time to leave but, I didn't because I had my own plan. I had to stay because the Pastor would be moving on soon and then the church would be mine. So in great discomfort I stayed waiting for the day he would be gone and I could take my rightful place, a place I was filling anyway as he had geographically moved away and was actually only Pastor in name only, but still the voice was leading me to leave. I told myself I would hang in there a few months till I was given the church. Everything would be good then I could follow the leading of the Spirit and everyone would be great. I had it all worked out. Well one day a leaders meeting was being called and I remember the voice kept repeating this name in my head again and again. Well the meeting started and next thing I know the World Bishop is zoomed in, and then it was said the new Pastor of church 2 was this name. The name that the Voice had been repeating in my head. I am grateful to the voice for giving me a warning. I was able to conceal my shock and maintain my dignity. Man oh man was I hurt and broken. I had totally forgotten that the voice had told me to leave but I stayed because of my own selfish desires. Was I done wrong in a manner of speaking? I think it could have been avoided if I had heeded the voice. It took me almost a year to heal from that hurt, but God knows how to heal his children. The question is do we know how to let him? I was wounded and bleeding all over my new Pastors and Overseer, they kept on loving, challenging and praying. Soon I started a new fellowship based on the vision God had given me in the middle of Corona. Yes, the Voice had released me, healed me and made me full of new hope. I made a lot of mistakes in the opening phase, made the mistake of putting trust in people and not consulting the Voice, but that's been taken care of and we are now about 2 years old. We are a small loving and caring fellowship. I heard the voice say these are enough to make them a firm foundation. Like I said the very first time I heard the voice I gave Him a yes again. I had to put away what my idea of what success looks like and trust the Voice. Now and again I notice that emptiness as before, but not as strong. The pull of ego, the pull of self, but I must crucify it because I cannot serve two masters. My Ego and my desires must not come before God. If I follow my ego and earthly desires I will end up in the same place that always lead me to great emptiness. The Voice will never fail you. I have learned to put away the plans and ways of man and to follow the Voice. The path has been hard at times but I have never been so at peace so full in the space that was once so empty.

Another thing that may be learned from my story is that a few times I thought I was there that I had arrived. Like when I was able to kick the drug and alcohol, I thought I was there but now I know it was just a step on the way, but at the time I thought it was everything that I was there. When God called me in Israel and I had found my first church I knew that was the end I was there. Then in church 2 with pastor and doing great works of healing and deliverance I knew then I had definitely arrived. I remember how I felt when I showed my picture on a poster announcing us in Russia. I remember him and I preaching a 3 day men's conference just the two of us carried by the Holy Spirit. Oh I have surely arrived having witnessed signs and wonders and having a few flow through me. I must have arrived but no. My destination is the great white throne of judgment and my goal is to hear the Voice say well done thy good and faithful servant. Until then everything else is just a great day of which I pray you will have many.

I Will Live and Not Die

Andrea Bernard

Life as we know it is shaped by a culmination of experiences, a formulation of activities from our inception to the point at which we cease to exist. Within this construct of activities and experience, our interaction with nature, our world, people create attachments; imprints in our mind, heart, body and soul. They create bonds. Bonds have a specific purpose and an appropriate time. Created too soon or too late or even in certain environments can have long standing destructive effects. Some ought never to come into existence.

This is an excerpt from Finding Fifty a Journey to Identity and Healing Through a Season of Abuse, a rough patch of life in the midst of being obedient to God. The goal is to make people aware of how toxic relationships can affect an individual and that there are people who truly desire no good for us. It is a reminder that even if we make a wrong turn, we can be restored. However this is also to remind us of the omnipotence and omnipresence of God in every situation life has to offer.

"But I will restore you to health and heal your wounds." Jeremiah 30:17

"Ma'am if this is not resolved and we have to come back, we will have to place both of you under arrest. So if you have the cord please return it so this matter can be settled" the male said. I had only been home about thirty minutes before a knock on the door revealed two uniformed officers responding to a domestic call regarding "stolen" property. My spouse spoke up, "Yes, I did made the call." I immediately assumed that something must have transpired while I was at work until I heard him explaining to them what took place. "So you see it was only she and I here and now my computer cord is missing....she is the only one that left since last night and it was here then."

The officer turned to me and said, "Ma'am can you tell us what happened"? Do you know anything about this and did you remove the computer cord?" I was shocked, in complete disbelief! "You need to tell the truth and give me back my computer cord" my spouse demanded as I was being questioned. "Sir, I don't even know what is going on right now. I do not have or have I even touched a computer cord or the computer. The only cord I ever touched was to plug the TV back into the wall after my spouse unplugged it while I was watching TV last night." After having me explain what transpired the night before, it was evident that the officers were becoming frustrated, especially with him interrupting and calling me a liar. This was not the first nor would it be the last of encounters with law enforcement arriving after being summoned to our dwelling place.

The journey to this place began as part of answering a call by God to move. I had moved out of state to a place I knew not nor did I know anyone at that time. This was an Abraham journey leaving my most precious treasure. Though I challenged it, God made it crystal clear that I had to go where He was sending me. There are twists and turns on the journey never anticipated. There are wrong turns we may make along the way. However even in the wrong turns, God NEVER left me alone.

My soul had made that determination long before my mind comprehended what that meant. Never would those words truly become life until I heard the still voice say "Get up and call the police." What had just happened!?? I picked up my body from the kitchen floor.

Searching for my phone to no avail, I entered my son's room, grabbed his phone and dialed 911. Waiting for officers to arrive, my body in pain and mind had not yet synchronized.

The officers arrived and soon questions began. I did not know that there was a scar on my face or hands. As he spoke, I prayed to God that the truth would be visible. It was visible enough for the officer and I remember the officer telling his partner to "Bangle him". Immediately this generated an automatic protective order. This was only a minuscule step in the next 5 year journey.

Could it really be, was this just a terrible nightmare? I would wake up soon right? The days and months that followed led me down a dark and lonely place. I believe that only those who have experienced similar happenings would relate. When emotional and/or verbal abuse becomes physical that space leaves an emptiness that words cannot fill and groans barely come.

My world had just been shaken something quite different. I remember being told that he had been bailed out late that evening and until the locks were changed I lived in pure fear constantly. Every footstep on the stairs outside, even the mail being delivered sent me into a panic. Except to pick the children up from work, I didn't leave the house for weeks fearing that he would appear at any given time. I only felt some relief whenever my son was home until the locks were changed.

Even still my mind was attempting to process what had transpired. I felt like this could not be real and at some point I would wake up from a terrible nightmare. I wanted him to hold me and tell me that I was dreaming. I wanted to still hear from him to make sense of it all. I wanted to hear him tell me it was a misunderstanding and that he was sorry. I wanted him to make it all better. I wanted him to tell me that we were going to be okay.

In the meantime, he never missed a beat going to church and had already begun to share a skewed story painting me as the culprit who called the police on him and had him arrested. When people began to call or text it was evident that apart from a select few most just wanted to be nosy. Upon my return to church I was constantly being asked about the whereabouts of my partner and more specifically, I remember one female church member telling me that "My brother (referring to my husband) would NEVER do that surely, you must have put yourself in the way to cause it!" Those inquiring knew only one version and about the protective order. A leader in the church even suggested that I have the order removed because it would not look good to have the police come there and that he should be free to come and worship without that being an issue.

Some cheerleaders made themselves very present and it was made to seem as if something was wrong with me, as if I had done something wrong while he took this as an opportunity to reside with a female parishioner who in no time boldly presented herself in a wife like state. He was shown sympathy and taken in with open arms while the opposite was true for me. My God, my God, my God!

There are many people who have experienced abuse and were further victimized by the very place that they expected would support them. Our churches are filled with people suffering silently because no one chose to believe them, and took the side of the abuser making assertions similar to what I was told. Some leaders are more concerned with pleasing the majority than speaking up for that which is wrong. In doing so, it is as if they choose to release Barabas time and time again just as we find in the account in Matthew 27:17. They turn a blind eye so as not to disrupt the flow of the church. This siding with the perpetrator, leaves the victim to be further abandoned and question themselves. Too often we are enamored by the look, title or position of an individual, never looking beyond the surface, even when time after time the voices of those closest to them are screaming out "HELP"! Eloquence of words, commitment to church service, members, activities, and consistency in tithe are great but where is the accountability to everyday Christ centered living? This is where some so-called "sanctified" soul will say we cannot pass judgment against others only God can, or all have sinned and come short, or he who is without sin let him cast the first stone. I implore you to explore God's scriptures thoroughly and allow the Holy Spirit to guide you in ALL truth! The Word of God is also for correction. We are called to hold each other accountable towards Godly living beyond the four walls of the church and it begins in how we treat those in our household first. My husband was able to continue as an officer exempt of correction.

Sometimes, I wished for a moment that I had a black eye or some other brutally visible scar that would prove to them an ounce of what I was experiencing, but I recognize that even such a bruise would have been taken out of context still in his support.

The response of the church perpetuated an internal rejection connected to a prior experience of exposure of being repeatedly sexually violated at an early point in my life and that perpetrator never being corrected by that church. The learned behavior for me out of these experiences was to shut up because obviously I nor my words held any value; it was okay to be abused in any capacity, molested by anyone, even violated. After all, I needed to just shut up and take it because the problem was inherently with me not the perpetrator(s)! How dare I accuse such a person in an office of position of being other than a God fearing, loving humble individual.

It has been explained to me in counseling by a psychologist that individuals skilled at this type of behavior keep a set of people in their corner at all times for the very purpose of being able to carry out every aspect of abuse, maintaining power and control at all times. The very act of bringing others into the conflict of the relationship is called triangulation. This can be done through flirting in front of you, infidelity, comparing you to others, or doing something in front of others that they know will cause you to respond unfavorably to make you look unstable or mean. They are skilled at manipulation, wooing the crowd in his/her favor. The persons with whom they are able to find favor always sees you as the adversary. These individuals are called "flying monkeys" because they aid in inflicting pain, insult, and confusion towards you, always siding with the other person. These flying monkeys are adept at carrying gossip, lingering around to watch for any opportunity to see your demise. Part of their purpose is to send you back into the arms of the abuser by making you think something is wrong with you.

During this season, I experienced a place of total depression and isolation. At one point as I stretched out on the living room couch one day the thought of suicide enveloped my mind. I could hear the enemy trying to convince me to just give up and end it. I felt like I could hardly breathe. My fingers shaking sent out a text to my covenant sisters with the words "Need prayer now". Each one resided in a different state but I can attest that over the next few minutes I was lulled into a sleep and when I awakened the suicidal thoughts had left. They did not even know what had taken place. "And it shall come to pass, that before they call, I will answer; and while they are yet speaking, I will hear" (Isaiah 65:24)

I started to doubt what had really transpired, the more I went to church. It was in outside counseling that reality was being presented to me and individuals were vying for my protection, safety and health emotionally, mentally and spiritually. However, at the time, I did not fully grasp this. I wanted it to come from the place I believed was supposed to love me.

There is an old saying I remember from childhood, "Sticks and stones may break my bones, but words will never hurt me." If you are around my age, you are pretty familiar with that saying. We chanted it so many times as children, however later a realization came that words can hurt. They can do more damage than the stick or stone in some instances causing deep wounds. Words are energy. Words have the power to orchestrate life and death. To create and to destroy.

"I don't want you! Get out of my apartment and out of my life. You are the worst mistake I have ever made in my life ever since the day I said I do. You are just like trash to me". Along with these words my clothes were pulled from the closet, and thrown all over the bedroom floor. The demeaning continued. My frame sat up in our bed with the Bible open on my lap as I silently read and prayed. A still small voice spoke to me saying "Peace be still, I promise you he will have to put every piece back in its place before the night is done. Watch...you will not have to speak once. Just continue to read my Word". The bantering continued for a little while longer followed up with "See what you made me do!" followed by the picking up of every piece of clothing being hung back in the closet, the closet door being shut and him going to take a shower.

My spirit chuckled. Inside I thanked my Daddy God, I closed my Bible, slid down into the bed pulling the covers up to my eyes, and smiled my way to sleep praising God yet in awe the whole time.

Verbal abuse especially from a loved one followed by such physical exertion such as described is designed to target one's self esteem and create fear within the individual. A person who once thrived in healthy self-confidence can overtime lose his/her identity. When our identity is stolen or misplaced it creates a breeding ground for negative strongholds to take root. However, God's hovering can soften the blow of the enemy.

The protection of our Creator far exceeds our comprehension. In hindsight, my physical existence could have been eliminated many times especially because I had been walking around with my eyes wide shut. The fact that many physical lives has been dissipated or even wiped out at the hand of their abuser is not to be taken lightly. Notwithstanding, the impact that emotional abuse leaves a hollowness similar to that of the vacancy of a soul from the body in a casket or one requiring resuscitation. I am grateful to exist in a revived status.

Laying in our bed on my husband's side, I felt the emptiness, the coldness and sense of loneliness in his absence. Is this what he meant? Was this what he was trying to express about my traveling?

The vibration of each sound was elevated and my body kept anticipating keys in the lock opening the front door with every footstep in the hallway outside our apartment. What would I do? What would I say? What would happen? He had told me that the apartment was not in a condition to enter and that there was a dispute with the landlord. He had sternly warned me not to go without him. What if she showed up.....my mind playing the variety of scenarios was abruptly interrupted by a thundering noise followed by the loud tone of a male voice, the sobbing of a female voice, and a baby crying (between 1-3yrs). The words and scenario so familiar to me. It was coming from upstairs directly above our bedroom! He was verbally devaluing her, demanding she respond and inflicting pain. The sound would get louder and there were instances of crashing tumbling sounds along with the sobbing and the baby crying. This torture continued for hours throughout the night with short spurts of silence. The police responded twice to the anonymous calls, but each time they knocked on the door there would be silence and no one answered.

The scene playing out above triggered a wealth of emotions throughout that night and the following day. As my frame at times froze, the familiar scenes in our marriage from its inception to that present moment played like a movie in my mind. It was not pretty, it was not joyful, it was not heartwarming, and it was the complete opposite. This was a slight awakening. No longer did the emptiness, coldness and sense of loneliness I initially felt in his absence reflect a possible point in my husband's favor, it reflected the truth about the status of the existing shell that housed my diminishing soul!

The part of my flesh was desiring that which was not good for me, but my inner spirit simply needed a refreshing reminder of the former to make a determination for the better. Verbal and mental abuse of any kind creates emotional trauma bonds within our minds making us at times believe that what our abuser tells us is truth. It strips us of true logic till we believe the skewed perceptions, consistently dismissing truth, instead favoring the lies our abuser instills in us. Oftentimes these lies are sealed through engaging us intimately, sexually. These are calculated, making us more prone to remaining and questioning our sanity. We begin to believe that we have overreacted or did not take into consideration his/her emotions, especially when we are "loved" following degradation. This causes us to "want" to get it right for him/her, in essence be approved.

What is phenomenal about the Creator is that He will not leave our soul in Sheol (hell). He will not allow us to stay in the pit or in darkness, but will reveal to us as many times as needed what it takes to save us or bring us out. "For you will not leave my soul in hell, neither will you allow your Holy One to see corruption. You will show me the path of life; In your presence is fullness of joy at your right hand are pleasures forevermore". (Act 2:27-28, Psalms 16:10-11) The Holy Spirit will lead us and guide us in ALL truth and bring back things to our remembrance. Simply confirming the need to accept my material losses, secure the necessary items and depart. Making a decision to leave everything behind and start all over is in no way easy. However, I am always reminded that material things are replaceable. You are not!

Though my journey began in answering a call from God, I could never have anticipated that I would find myself in a relationship that would cause as much destruction to my being as this one. However, what I can attest to is that in every step of this mess that I found myself in, God made himself present and his protection kept me safe despite the fire(s) all around me. Even in my misstep, God NEVER allowed me to be alone whether I felt it or not. He created a safe exit yet ensured that HIS calling was fulfilled. Through the daily work I had been sent to do, his mission was accomplished. Please understand that I am not endorsing that anyone remain in a relationship that is toxic.

I often questioned this journey especially having endured the abusiveness. Since my return, the specificity of this journey has been confirmed many a times. I learned a plethora of things about myself, my belief, my faith, marriage, and relationships.

The journey through the fire required of me a strong will to live, a deep trust and relationship with my Creator, ongoing prayers, a few good counselors and therapists trained in the behaviors I experienced, a circle of safety, but most of all the willingness to look in the mirror at the good, bad, and ugliness. I would not have made it through if I didn't tap into the resources and help available. There was some searching required. There was listening required. Separation from people, places, and things had to occur. There were many tears and I really had to unlearn some unhealthy behaviors by replacing them with healing/healthy ones. I had to take ownership for my part. Yes, there is a work that is required of each one of us if we are to thrive past the fire. I had to realize my self-worth. YES, that I AM WORTHY of honor, respect, love and so much more!

Some of us are still attempting to maneuver life from a wounded place. In order for the wound to properly heal, you have to take the bandages off at some point. At some point it needs to be exposed to fresh air to properly heal. However there is help and hope when we are ready to address instead of dressing the wound. This is a process not for the faint of heart, but for the courageous one willing to go through the fire. The promise as found in Jeremiah is restoration of health and healing of the wounds.

"But I will restore you to health and heal your wounds." Jeremiah 30:17, But you too must decide to live and not die.

Can You Hear Me Now?

_____

Russell & Joni Waller

When our coach and editor reviewed our first writing she asked us, what was our purpose for wanting to write about Relationships and communication? She said to us this sounds like the Huxtables. You had no struggles and no reconciliations? This made me think about the reason that I wanted to write about marriage. You see I've looked at our married life through my lenses and I've always felt there's got to be some more and if I find it I want to help other couples to love, laugh and realize that you can make it. You see it's always been a passion for me to be able to help someone not experience unnecessary bumps and bruises along the way.

I don't believe there is perfect marriage, because we are not perfect people. I believe we will see the perfect marriage is in Heaven. I do believe in the old song "If I Can Help Somebody Along the Way, Then My Living Shall Not Be in Vain." If Russ and I can help somebody heal or realize that their marriage is not so different from any other marriages, that the struggles of life are going to be there, but you're going to get to the other side if you stick it out and hang in there, then our marriage has not been in vain. If we can tell you that your marriage is always going to evolve because you're growing, and "hang in there baby!" Then our marriage has not been in vain. If we can give you some tidbits and give you a glimpse into our married life to let you see that love changes and Metamorphosing as you go along, then our marriage has not been in vain! So this is really why we wrote about our experiences. We want to help other couples, to let them know they're not alone in their struggle and some of what you may be experiencing is the normal progression of two people who did not grow up together come together and live as one.

This writing is a compilation of both of our ideas on marriage. In its beauty you will see two different styles of writing our thoughts on communication to you which in the end will merge and marry into a beautiful idea of what we, Russell and Joni, think of the importance of communication and how we fluidly have learned to communicate as a couple.

A Question for You:

Does how you learned to communicate in your family (as a child) determine how you learn to communicate effectively with others, and possibly could it be an influence on how you have to relearn to communicate with others?

A Love Story

When asked to contribute to the book, I, Joni thought, "What could I/we possibly have to offer others?" It was said to us in 40 + years of marriage you should have some possible advice and tips on communication and nuggets. Well, let me tell you this assignment has been a journey full of self-discovery, discovery of what communication is and how I personally communicate with my spouse and others. First of all I don't know how two people who grew up so differently came together as one to share their life as a whole. I am an only child (me-female) and my husband (the oldest of five) "KABOOM!"

Joni's Love Story

Well, here we are 40 plus years!" A statement you may hear throughout this writing! Wow, looking back over the 40+ years of marriage is an interesting camera shot. It's been a journey from the time Russell asked me to marry him until the time I said I do. Well here's our story. Although Russell and I dated for two years and he had asked my parents particularly, my dad, for their blessing to marry me, I remember vividly, my dad telling me from the house, to the limo, to the church "You know you don't have to do this!" Matter fact now that I think about it, he was saying it as we were walking down the church aisle! Lol! His question to me was not because he did not like his son-in-law to be, but because he knew the struggles of marriage and particularly a young marriage. He knew that there were going to be some struggles and some hardships along the way. He wasn't sure if we were prepared and equipped mentally, and financially to handle them, especially since we had just come out of college! I was still in the college mindset of dating my soon to be husband, Russell. We laugh now because my dad said "I'll give you a car if you wait a year!" Wow can you believe it, we could've had a brand new car to ride around in and a new marriage! But No, we took door number two and dived into marriage head first! LOL!

So we're just going to dive right in as I said. The night before we got married, I had my poor Pastor sitting for an hour trying to find a wedding vow that I would agree to say, because the word "obey" was in the vow. And I, Joni, take my relationship with God very seriously and I said to my Pastor I can't agree to obey to him and the only person I was going to obey was God. My poor attendants, they sat in the church not knowing what was going on behind the scenes. However, my Pastor did find a vow that I would agree to because he knew me and of my strong convictions to God.

I mentioned this story because we did not have marital counseling before we got married. We didn't have counseling on how to communicate with each other, we didn't have counseling on financial obligations to each other and businesses, and we didn't have counseling on whatever one would get from Spiritual God Lead Marriage Counseling from a Pastor. I was finishing college in Virginia and Russell had finished the year before me and was teaching in Virginia. Now don't get me wrong, we had wonderful parents who stayed in the game of marriage for many years and were great examples to us. However, their concern was a little different for us. They had longevity and experience, they had built a strong marriage foundation through the ups and downs. They knew what it took to make a good marriage and they knew the whimsical feeling of two young lovers, (Russell and I) on our wedding day would only last so long.

We had a beautiful wedding ceremony and honeymoon. So after the honeymoon, here we are off to a running start in our marriage! Where are we going? How are we getting there? Your guess was as good as ours! We knew we were going somewhere!!! My assumption of marriage and what it turned out to be, was a big eye opener. I thought I was going to be carried off into the sunset and live happily ever after!

You Like This? I Don't!

From the beginning I didn't realize how different we were because we had the same moral values and love for family. After all my family was from the south! But I was a city girl raised in the north and my husband was a farm kid (as he would say) raised in the south! Well, we moved back down south, (we met in college in Virginia) and I thought we were going to live in an apartment, but my husband put us in a small farm house. I wanted to buy a red MG sports car (My dream car from those 60's movies!). From those two differences alone, I realize now many times we were making individual decisions, but not making them together. This caused a lot of unnecessary heartache.

Russell didn't express to me his full reason for wanting to move into that farm house, just that the rent was cheap, his vision was to save money for the future and a house. He also said we needed a large car for traveling because our families lived 5 hours away from us (still wanted my red MG). Maybe he did express his reasoning the moves he thought would be beneficial for us, but I just wasn't paying attention because I am a pleaser at heart, so I just went along with it! The lesson here is you should know yourself and listen for understanding.

I knew full well, that was not my speed, I agreed to all of this! Furthermore I was in love! What could go wrong? The house was old and there were no young people my age living around us (how about that). Don't get me wrong, there were nice people living around us, but they were older! I hid my disappointment and tried to live through it not expressing my overwhelming unhappiness to my new husband because I was in love! I should have had the courage to tell him how unhappy I was. I thought he could see it just because he loved me! Everyone else could see it, my aunt and uncle wouldn't even come back to visit us anymore because I cried every time they left to go up north!

The lesson here is that couples should speak up and tell their truth! Because I wouldn't speak up I believe it started to bring an insecurity of how I viewed myself! Somewhere along the line I think I grew up thinking I had to be kind to everyone and to put their needs before mine. Thank goodness I'm not like that now!!! I mean I am still kind of! I just recognize that my self-worth is extremely important!

As I stated, I am very family oriented and I needed to go home more often, but I learned that young love, working and finance don't always mix well. So I tried to stick it out which made me feel unhappy in the marriage, but once again, I didn't really express my strong need to go home to Russell, so he had no clue of how I was feeling! You've got to communicate those feelings! So I stayed until I could not bare it any more. I went home for the summer or so Russell thought. Boy, when I tell you, one loving father wanting to know why I was home so long and two praying mother in laws who loved each other and their children got together something happens! They made us realize that everyone doesn't have a supportive in law unit like we have. They talked to both of us making no judgment of who was right or wrong, just that we had to learn to communicate. My grandmother, another loving influence on our marriage, who took no sides when we both would come to her to plead our case, with Mother...would said "There are three sides to a story, "Mine, Yours and the Truth in the Middle!" This meant children go back and figure it out as a couple. So, Russell and I came up with the start of a plan for a solution for my unhappiness. We moved back to my home area on the condition that he found a job up here. Guess what? Job found!!!

The Beginning of a New Problem!
Well, we moved out of a brand new house that we had built from the ground up in the last year. I recently, found out after 42 years of marriage that his thinking was when we had children he wanted to bring them from the hospital into a house. But, being young and in love, once again that wasn't a conversation we even

54

thought to have. We sold that house and moved back up North, as I stated earlier. We comprised, but my husband was not a happy camper! A brand new house and great jobs! You can imagine, that was something we had to work through. Now the roles were reversed, one happy person and one unhappy person. So now we had to work through this. I don't know how we did it, there were so many long discussions about the sacrifices we made for each other and some finger pointing along the way. I think our love for each other out weighed our frustration or maybe we had frustrated love! One thing I know for sure is that we are God's children and He gently stuck by us saying "You can make it children!" But when I look back now "I think who those two young people were?" Those were some frustrating days! With God's help we pushed through and got through it AND you will too!!

Lesson here- Know yourself and listen for understanding.

By the way who did I marry?

Pay attention to who you are marrying. What do I mean? Study your spouse. Find out about them while you are dating. What's your favorite food or movie? What do you like to do in your spare time? What are your favorite activities or hobbies? Who's one of your best friends or favorite family members? Perhaps all of these questions you can get more clarity and information on who this person is you are marrying!

Joni's Ice Cream Story and other Sweet Tooth Stories

One day when we were traveling from Petersburg to Richmond, I saw an ice cream truck and said to Russell something like "There's an ice cream truck." I think he responded like oh ye-ah" and we drove on past. I was disappointed! By now, you have listened to me tell some of our journey of love, so you might have an inclination of who I am. How do you think I should have responded? How did I respond? You got it, we drove right on by with me not saying a word and being angry with myself because I didn't express that I really, really wanted to get ice cream.

Lesson here- Validate yourself, you have a voice you can use it.

After dating a while, my husband still had a few lessons to learn about me when it came to sweets. We were still in the dating mode and we were coming out of the drugstore. I had bought a Hershey's chocolate bar, I was about to enjoy all to myself! Mmm! Well, Russell asked if he could have a piece. Remember, I'm an only child with a sweet tooth, and I'm a little selfish when it comes to my sweets. I will share, but, I only have one vice, "Not when it comes to sweets!" Now, back to my comment, "I will share", which I did! I went back in the store and I bought him, his own candy bar!

Back to my original comment, study your spouse, and know who they are. My husband, has learned me. He knows I have an attachment to sweets and will tell you if you give Joni a choice between a piece of chicken or a slice of cake, she'll choose the cake every time!

Lesson here- Embrace who you are and embrace who your spouses is.

In Sickness and in Health

The times when you have to lean on each other is the true test of the strength of the relationship. It is when you develop or find the strength of love the relationship is built on. It is when you learn to lean on each other for support and where you'll let the vulnerable side of life be shown. After all we are human, we have hurts, insecurities and life's pain at time in our lives.

You've heard the expression "Life is a journey and not a sprint!" It is a journey! There will be some bumps and bruises along the way. There's going to be some unexpected turns along the way. There's going to be some life-changing events along the way, some sickness and health problems along the way, as well as times when you have to cry in the midnight hour because of the loss of a loved one along the way. In this 40 + year journey we've had tears of joy and sorrow. We were both blessed to have our fathers in our lives to show us what almost 60 years of marriage looks like, but I tell you when your parent passes away, you're still a child and it hurts no matter how old you are. Russell and I loss both of our fathers within a year of each other. This is when the true test of knowing your spouse really comes in handy because the grieving process is hard enough in itself. You have to know your spouse enough to know when they need support and comfort and when they need space and private time. My husband knew when I needed to cry it out and I knew what it meant when he was in his quiet space.

There were times when one of us decided to visit the hospital to have children (lol) or have surgery or just an observation visit. Russell was right there being an attentive nurse after I came home with a child, both times. He was up just as much as I was day and night. He helped care for each new born even though he had to get up and go to work the next day. The same thing when I had surgery. He was right there attending to my needs and I'm sure he was exhausted. I also remember a time when Russell had to have an overnight stay in the hospital for observation. When that happens they don't give you a choice to go home and pack your bags and then come back to the hospital. No, they are keeping you right then. Well after being thoroughly checked out they sent him upstairs to a room. You all know I was not going to leave my husband and go home. So I, Joni, spent the night in the hospital family room on a couch that was probably 4 feet by 3 feet. I'm 5'1 so it was a BIT uncomfortable, but I was not going to leave my husband's side. I slept on that couch so I could be near him and also so I could talk to any medical personnel that had to do with his condition. By the way, he thought it was chest pain, but it was drinking ice cold water after working outside in extreme heat! Thank the Lord it was only that! Which leads me to a thought, we have to be concerned about each other's health and well-being! When I look at my husband now, I see his kindness towards me and others. He's a genuine brother! There are many other things we've been through but would probably be a volume in itself!

Working on Myself

I stated earlier, my husband and I grew up differently, so there are times when we saw finances differently, because, he is the oldest our views of money are different even to the smallest of things! It's funny we have NO problems agreeing when it comes to big purchases! There are times when we are together shopping and the comment of the cost of items price comes up, to me it makes me feel like he's saying I'm not worth what he's spending. Now I know better than that! My response is to express how it makes me feel, loudly, as if he's deaf! To me, in my mind, I heard "That's too much money for you or me to spend," Knowing my husband, he's just making a comment not an attack on my self-worth. However, I took my perception of his comment personally. This in turn made me rethink my response later, with an apology. (Loudness wasn't necessary!) As I think back to past conversations, there were so many times I could have responded differently, for instance I could have asked, why did you say that? Or why do you think that? I may have gotten a response to his underlying thought process which may have avoided a communication mishap.

Russell's Love Story

First, I give all Praise, Honor and Glory to my Lord and Savior Jesus Christ. Just a little background on this young man named Russell Wyatt Waller. I was born in the small town of Danville, Virginia, predominantly a blue collar working class community in the south western part of Virginia. With me being the oldest of five children, three beautiful young ladies and two handsome young men, I have always felt in charge of my four siblings. I felt that it enabled me to constantly work on my communication skills. Being the oldest also put me in a position to make authoritative decisions, which I carried in to my marriage. My father was a very hard working young man that always had a strong entrepreneur spirit. He was the oldest of two, himself and one sister. He was able to attend public school through the sixth grade. His entrepreneur spirit enabled him to successfully work two occupations for most of his adult life. Later, in quest to fulfill his dream of entrepreneurship he worked successfully as a tobacco farmer for nearly 45 years. My father was a great communicator because of his kind easy going spirit. My mother, on the other hand was a proud graduate of the class of 1957, Southside High School in Danville, Virginia. She was a wife, mother of 5 children and a great homemaker. She was the oldest of 11 children, 10 beautiful young ladies and one handsome young man. My mother always encouraged us to work hard and learn to become self-sufficient in our life endeavors. I attributed her great communication skills to her being the oldest sibling. My parents were married in holy matrimony on December 26, 1956 at the ages 23 (dad) and 18 (mom). From very early in our lives our parents instilled in us many of the "Golden Rules"- 1. Honesty is the best policy, 2. Treat others like you would like to be treated, 3. Be a man or woman of your word, and 4. Practice what you preach (Love sisters, brothers and others as Christ loved the Church). They were very good communicators as we were going through different stages of our lives, and because of their belief in the Lord Jesus Christ and their strong convictions in Him, they made directions, rules and guidelines very easy to follow. They always tried very hard to equally divide up the sibling tasks. My parents were faithful in taking us to the family's Baptist churches for Sunday worship services, Sunday School, choir rehearsals, Homecomings, Bible Study, etc. These activities greatly enhanced our growth and development in communication. One thing I know for sure "Our parents passed down great work ethics and integrity in us!"

The Young Years

From the very early years of my life. I have always wanted to meet a young lady that would love me as much as I would love her. I tried working on this major task without involving God, but I soon discovered that this task must involve God. I always watched my parents move along through their lives loving, working, and caring for each other in such a calm peaceful manner. They were strong believers in the Lord. They constantly would reference God in their various daily activities. My parents like other married couples would show differences of opinions about various situations, but always managed to come up with a solution. During certain trials, I could hear my mother in her quiet way praying to God on her husband's and children's behalves. I truly believe that they never made decisions without talking to God, even though I didn't always hear them praying and talking to God, but I know they did!

It All Began On the Block

It all began in the fall of 1979 on the beautiful campus of Virginia State University in Petersburg, Virginia. This is where I found a beautiful young princess named Joni Vanessa McNair. Little did I know that I was staring right at the young lady that would become the future Mrs. Russell W. Waller. After all, Saturday football games, win or lose, students would gather to meet each other before dinner. This main campus of VSU would become stage for great block shows hosted by various members of the Greek Organizations. This was a very big campus event for the Greek lettered Sororities, Fraternities and Social Organizations at this particular time of the school year. The Block Shows were held in front of Virginia Hall across from the main university dining hall. It seemed if everyone had the same idea and that was to come up to the block an observe the Greek and Social groups preform their fancy routine step shows and just simply meet and greet each other to talk.

I didn't realize at the time that the young lady that was so beautiful, which such a radiant smile that succeeded in catching my undivided attention was Ms. Joni McNair from New Jersey. When I cut my eyes around to get a better view of her over all of the people that were there she was staring right at me and just smiling. I remember like it was yesterday. Joni's smile was infectious. Since I was such a cool and collective "Big" transfer Senior on campus who was in her brother fraternity, I tried my best to pretend as if I wasn't even looking at her, even though I followed her every move. She was so cute and dainty wearing her sorority paraphernalia. Little did I know that I was starting at my future bride, the mother of our children and love of my life.

Days later I began to see Joni around the campus and my mind immediately went back to how I felt about her when I first laid eyes on her. Not only did I see her around campus attending various classes, but I made a point to be wherever she was, wherever I thought she'd be coming out of. If she had a health class, I made it my business to be at the gymnasium or somewhere on the second floor, where she literally had to walk right into me. I wonder if she knew that what I was doing would be considered "stalking!" I would consider it being very fond of her! She would give me a pleasant "hello" and smile and that would fan the fire even more. Then we began to run into each other in the cafeteria. I wanted to approach her, so bad in the "Caf," as we called it, but I was intimidated by her and so bashful that I would not approach her. So I just tried to continue to be there whenever I thought she would be there. Then one day she approached the table I was sitting at and asked me if anyone was using the seat next to me, so I said no one was sitting there. I was so happy and my heart started racing. (I didn't realize at the time, that her best friend who I knew, told her that I liked her and to my surprise she was interested in me too!). I was thinking to myself, "Wow I get to meet her and talk to her." That day we had a very good conversation. We began to talk and share things, little did I know that she was dating another young man, eventually that came to an end. I was so happy, I still tried to be wherever she was coming out of class though! Later during that year we began to see more of each other. I have to admit I was trying to get to see more of Joni, but I also was trying to see another young lady and I forgot to mention that I had a girlfriend at home as well! But, I have to admit, Joni was still on my mind. I felt very badly, and my weekend home trips began to be fewer, but I had to go home and break the news that I had found someone. I was so happy to get back to campus. I couldn't wait to see Joni. I'd been thinking about her the entire winter break.

So This Is Marriage!
When I thought of marriage, I thought of a beautiful young lady and a very handsome young man meeting each other and

going through a reasonable amount of time dating and getting to know each other. I felt that this beautiful couple would become engaged and become totally committed to each other and learn to share all the great and wonderful things that God had provided for them, such as an everlasting friendship, happiness, peace and understanding, togetherness, agape love, children, family, a home, and Christian values and beliefs in our Lord and Savior Jesus Christ. Our home would be built and shared by two beautiful young people in a Holy covenant blessed by God, committing themselves to each other through good times, sickness, great health, bad health, great discussions, bad/heated discussions, home management, family planning, child care, child management, career planning, and etc.

Early in our marriage we decided to relocate from Fredericksburg, Virginia to Lawrenceville, New Jersey. It was a very difficult time for me. The difficulty in this relocation decision was caused because I believed in my heart that we were on the path of building a future for our family in the Fredericksburg, Virginia area. We had just moved into our new home in Fredericksburg and now nearly 8 months later we are moving to New Jersey. I felt in my heart that the plan we had made together had taken a different turn and caused a totally different outcome on the plan that we had worked out together. So this a prime example of not communicating and being on the same page, but looking back with much prayer, misunderstanding of a lack of communication and coming to some kind of resolution, we got it together.

Our Takeaways from Coming to the Table of Communication

Let's Dive In!

What is Communication? The dictionary states that it is "the imparting or exchange of information or news," "the successful conveying or sharing of ideas and feelings," "social contact" and several more with the same idea meaning of the above stated.

To me, Joni, Communication begins with being transparent with each other. It begins with being transparent and vulnerable. Hoping those thoughts and feelings you share or about to share will be understood an accepted. It begins with going deep inside your soul. It begins with the main part, which is inviting the Holy Spirit to sit down at the table with you, to guide your tongue, open your ears and your heart so that you can truly hear and accept each other's perspective. It means really listening to each other at the table (we'll talk about that later), and coming together so that solution(s) can be created. It means dealing with hard situations.

As I thought about getting to the table, I knew I needed to seek God. God was saying to me work on yourself. Through pray and meditation, I realized that I had some work to do as it related to Joni. What did I need to recognize within me to be a better communicator? Self-Love and Clarity of Mind. I realized that I devalued my own contributions to the conversation (this one is not just for marriage).

*So here's a sidebar- Stop being intimidated by what you think people think of you, validate your own feeling! If you are not sure of who you are, how can you bring your concerns clearly and confidently to the table? When you come to the table knowing who you are it makes a world of difference in how you respond and the response you will receive. It will also help with the outcome you and your a spouse are trying to achieve.

Communication Tip:
-Remember know who you are and bring your concerns clearly and confidently! (Again, loudness isn't necessary!)
-Asking a question may help for better clarification!

Getting to the Table
So how do you get to the Table Talk of Communication? This is going to depend on the vision you and your spouse share as one unit and what the table looks like to both of you. How about this, you set a weekly, bi-weekly or monthly check in, or whatever you

choose. I would **not** suggest doing it 2 or 3 times a week, you've got to give life a chance to happen during the week. (Now, I'm not saying if there are pressing issues you wait until its table talk time. You have to deal with the issues of daily living.) Your table talk could be a, "How are we doing this week? Do we have any shared concerns? Or do you have any concerns that I am not aware of?

Well, where should this table talk be you ask? Certainly Not in the bed!!! I would say find a neutral place in the house, a place that brings peace. You could even play some soft music. How about going to the park, taking a drive, or sitting outside on a nice day. Ohhh! Just thought of this one, sitting at the fire pit in the evening! Don't forget a pencil, pad, paper, calendar etc. you may need those to help you stay accountable to each other,

Communicating properly is growth! What do I mean? When you can leave the table with both of you feeling a sense of working together, that's growth! When you both can look back and see how you were able to get over that hurdle and come to a solution, that's growth! Oh, but did I mention that God has to be the first one at the table! You have to meet Him there. As a matter of fact, you have to ask Him to meet you there! You have to spend time with Him individually in prayer, sharing your concerns with Him, before you come to the table. God needs to be the third strand cord in the relationship. That 3 strand cord, you've heard of that! Singer Erica Campbell song quotes, "I need a life line right now, 911 won't do...Lord it's me this time. Help, I just can't make it if I don't have your Help."

So, what am I saying? We often go into the conversation ready to talk, explain, give our opinion, share our side, and/or have both barrels blazing in preparation for a fight before we seek the help of the Helper. The one who can sooth voice tones for listening, the one who can open our ears for listening, the one who can open our hearts for receiving. Who is that one? God, seek Him first before you go to your communication table/room etc., so you won't come out with unnecessary battle scars. This may sound harsh but husbands, truth be told, we wives don't really like drama that comes with settling problems, we want solutions and actions. We all should try a little tenderness.

Getting to the Other Side of 40 +Years and Still Working on It

Whew! Because we keep struggling with the same issues at times, it's hard to see how to get to the other side some times. We are not perfect. We are human! I'm still learning my spouse and he's still learning me. We grow and we grow up in marriage. Does that make sense to you? What I am saying is that daily we are growing and learning something new about life, however through life's journey as a married couple, we grow up, we matured, our likes and dislikes change and we have evolved into a new people. Russ and I are not the young 22 and 21 year old who got married with little experience in life. We've learned a few things about each other and about marriage.

So, how did the Wallers make it to 40+ years? Well it's a journey. Learning to communicate effectively with each other keeps us on a continuum of education of who this person is that I married. Learning each other's love language was important. For me, learning that I'm not going to hurt my husband's feelings if I express how I feel about something that we may vehemently disagree on. (I, for some reason, felt intimidated sharing my real feelings on an issue, I don't know why. Perhaps it was being an only child, not having to have or learn the art of negotiation. I didn't have anyone but myself to have a dispute with!), but after 40 years how would he know how I felt about something if I didn't share my true thoughts and feelings. If I didn't share my thoughts and feelings about my true self how would he ever know the real woman he was marrying,

I love to laugh and have fun and have often try to use humor as a way to deal with various situations. Russell on the other hand is more serious and to the point. One time I had a dream and, I woke myself up telling stand-up comedy to my classmates when I was in high school! Remember I said "This was only a dream!" In reality I held back and was afraid to show Russell that side of me. I didn't share this part of me when we first met, the fun loving comedian! It was a hidden, underdeveloped talent that was always there. I didn't learn to express who I was early on because I was still evolving. Had I expressed who I knew me to be at that time to my future husband, it might have not caused me so much internal struggle and bought more laughter to our table talks while we were learning to solve problems. But, 40 years later the grown up in me showed up, the one carrying around frustration of not knowing how to express my true self came barreling out! Sorry Husband! You'd think after buying several homes, 2 children, grandchildren, job losses, job gains, financial ups and downs and other life experiences we would be experts on how to get it right and communicate effectively so everyone comes away from the table blissfully happy? No! So what we have done and still do is, we work on our marriage by taking advantage of marriage retreats. Do we get it right after that? Still No! As I've stated before, communication is an ongoing process because we are always changing. But we've grown up from the young, young, young 20's couple. To help you with the elephant in the room you can guess how old we are! This should tell you that married life is a journey and communication is a process.

What we can share with you are some keys to Communicate we've learned along the way. May they be a blessing to you.

Keys to Communication
Pray before you discuss things or situations!
1. Come to the table to discuss only the issue at hand.
2. "No Tit for Tat!" That's a method of deflection and does not solve any problems.
3. Come to the table with a solution, but be open to your spouse's solution.
4. Set a timeline or completion date for things discussed to be completed, and then come back for a review or readjustment time if needed.

5. Set a "How Are We Doing?" Check In. This can be weekly, monthly or a timetable of your choice. This can be a time to share your thoughts and or feelings on the relationship. A "Tune Up," if you will! (We are still working on this one!)?

6. Find time to dance!!! Dancing provides that intimate connection that couples need to share! That's communication, right? (Still working on this one!)

7. Find things to laugh about! (Watch a movie or share a memory, have a hardy laugh!) Laughter restores the body!!

8. Don't use sex as a weapon and a way to get a problem solved. That doesn't work it only creates two unhappy, unfulfilled people.

9. Saying "I'm Sorry" goes a long way, if you truly mean it.

10. If an issue can't be resolved and is frustrating right then, leave if on the table, knowing you'll come back to it. Set a new time for discussion and return to it then. Return to it!!!

11. Remember you can't make anyone do anything, but you do have the power to ask.

Patience- Patience means listening without formulating your response while your spouse/partner is sharing their opinion or thoughts.

12. I said it before number 1- Pray separately and together on issues before you discuss them. Pray for clarity, peace, understanding and an open mind before you discuss everything at the table, (Where ever you table is!) Remember Prayer Changes Things! It changes Hearts!

Great Communication

Great communication can and is an extremely important tool to place in your marriage toolbox. Two very different people are coming together with the purpose of using skills and experiences that they have acquired in real life situations to convey to one another their feelings and understandings about various circumstances that are constantly arising in marriage. They have to be very open-minded about the day to day occurrences that take place in their marriage.

A couple has to be very honest with each other, and willing to share their deepest thoughts and feelings at various times even though timing may not be conducive to the situation. They must learn to become good listeners by listening to their spouse's heart beat! So what do I mean by that? Listen to your spouse with a compassionate ear and always placing them in total consideration. If you can learn to have the ability to manage your feelings and emotions about many different topics at one time this will be a great skill set.

Marriage has to be built on a solid foundation of "Agape" building blocks. In Christianity, agape is unconditional love, the highest form of love. Agape is charity, the love of God for man and the love of man for God. Being able to communicate this type of love to your spouse is not always an easy task! Remember, marriage is made up of two individuals coming together in order to live as one! In closing remember "A couple must keep three people involved in their marriage thought pattern at all times." The number one person is God! The couple makes up the unity of the second and third people. Thank you, the reader, for going on this wonderful eye opening journey with us!

Love for the Game

Alexander J. Tillery

October 31, 1990 we went out to go trick or treat. Who would have known that would be the last night I would see her. I was thirteen when my mother passed away in her sleep. We returned home after trick or treating and I was excited about how much candy I had received. That night when I went to bed I had this crazy dream. In the dream I was getting up for school like I normally do. My mom would be up before me. In the dream when I woke up and went towards the bathroom I could hear my mother's alarm going off. There was only one bathroom in our condo and to get to it I had to walk through my mom's bedroom. As I walked to the bathroom there was a divider that blocked her bed for privacy. I go into the bathroom and when I come out I call her "Mom", "Mom wake up". I didn't get any response, so I go over to her bed to wake her up. I tapped her and said "wake up", but still no movement. I started screaming "mommy", then I woke up breathing heavy like I was out of breath. Who would have known that the dream I had would come to reality?

That morning November 1st 1991, my dream was real. I got up just like I did in my dream and went to the bathroom. My mom's alarm was going off and I called out to her and she didn't answer. I shook her to wake her up and she didn't move. I can still remember the song that was playing on her alarm clock. The lyrics "You wake up suddenly, you're in love". I didn't know at the time who sung that song. The crazy thing is, in the mist of me calling 911 for help. In my head I thought the lyrics were "Wake up suddenly, you're above". As I'm on the phone with 911, the lady asked me to get a mirror to put it under her nose to see if she was breathing and she wasn't. I called my sister Brenda after I got off the phone with 911. When they got there, I was in the living room. My sister arrived a few minutes after. I sat in my living room area and played my Nintendo the whole time the coroners were there. As they were bringing out her body in a bag, that is when I broke down crying. I couldn't believe she was gone. My mother and I were just starting to build that relationship to where I felt comfortable talking to her about anything. My mother and I always had a loving relationship, but as a young man, there were things I didn't want to talk to my mother about. That night I went to my sister's house, and I cried all night long. I couldn't eat or sleep, I just kept crying. My brother was locked up at the time my mom passed. My sister and I made the funeral arrangements together.

The day of the funeral I was numb. I was in a fog and didn't say much to anyone. At the end of the service I was asked to walk up to the casket to say my last goodbyes. I couldn't do it, and it is something that I wish I would have done. To see her face one last time before they closed the casket forever. I don't even remember the repass and who was there. The next few days I stayed home from school because I didn't want to be bothered. The first day I returned to school I got into a fight and bust a kid's nose. I don't even remember how it started, but all I could remember was he said "your mom". When I heard that I lost it, and my hands started to flow, connecting with so much anger and rage. I ended up getting suspended for four days for the fight, which to me was good because I wanted to be alone. My sister gave me a pass because she knew I was going through a lot. The next four days I stayed in my room, crying and playing my video game. I barely ate anything; I didn't want to go outside with my friends. I was depressed and scared, I didn't know what was going to happen. I didn't know how I would live without my mommy.

Then one day my friend James came to my house and told me about a basketball tryout. I didn't want to go; I didn't feel like doing anything. My sister and James talked me into going and that decision changed my life. I went to the tryouts in a pair of light blue jeans, white t-shirt, and blue Nike sneakers. I remember the first day of tryouts all we did was run, monkey drills, suicides, and laps the whole time. When I got home, I passed out, I don't remember if I even ate dinner. The next day was some of the same and I ended up making the team. I wasn't the most skilled player but the coach liked how I played defense and hustled. Basketball would change my life that day and moving forward.

Basketball became the way I dealt with my feeling, depression, and anger. Whenever I felt sad, angry or alone I turned to the game of basketball. That was the only time I felt safe or alive. I believe it is because it's a team sport and I needed others to play. I was so excited that I made the team all I did every day was play basketball. The more I played the more interested I got in it. It was to the point that I made my middle school basketball team. I was also able to play basketball at the high school level. Throughout high school I had a decent career. Because of basketball I was able to graduate high school. Many of times I wanted to drop out and go hustle for fast money, but I knew I wouldn't be able to play ball. The only way I was able to play basketball was to keep my attendance up and grades good. The game of basketball was like a drug for me. It was the way I could keep my mind busy and not think about my mom or my situation. I remember I had gotten in trouble at home and my sister Brenda told me I couldn't play in a big game. My team was sponsored by Nike so we all had team sneakers. My sister took my sneakers so I couldn't play that night. When I say it was like a drug, I had to play so I snuck out the house to play, but wait what I didn't mention was Brenda worked at the high school I attended. I didn't care about the consequences. I showed up to the game in all black sneakers while the whole team wore white. I just couldn't be denied the chance to play.

I would play every day. Sometimes I would have three games in one day. I would have a high school game at 4pm, leave there to play in a recreation league at 6:30 and finally play my last game at 9pm in another recreation league. I loved the game so much, that at the age of 17 I started coaching youth basketball. I would coach my 16 and under team and later that day play with my 18 and under team. I didn't see myself playing basketball at the next level.

One thing I did was make a promise to my mother that I would graduate high school. Basketball allowed me to keep that promise. After I graduated from high school, I did many things I wasn't proud of and I'm sure my mother wouldn't be as well. I tried to start out my next chapter in a positive way. I started working as a carpenter for a union. I was attending carpentry school to learn the trade. I would go to work and, on the days, I had class take a train ride from The Bronx down to West 4th Street in Manhattan. On those days of class I would see guys outside playing basketball. I would play a couple of games before class. If I saw or heard a ball bounce I wanted to play. I ended up moving out of my sister's house and got an apartment with my two cousins. I was working on construction projects and making good money. I was working on different site when I first got started. I would work one month on this site then two or three months on another. Everything was going well until, one of the construction projects was completed. When that happens, you go on a job list with the union and wait to be called for the next job available. Unfortunately for me I didn't have enough work history to collect unemployment. I wasn't worried because the union was getting jobs for guys within a week of finishing a project. My union had merged with another local union. This union was bigger and covered a large area of Manhattan. I thought this would be a good thing, but I didn't realize that because that union was bigger, means more members. That pushed me to the bottom of the list and there were a lot for guys out of work. I couldn't find work for 8 months and that was a low time for me in my life. I couldn't collect unemployment and I had no money coming in. I would borrow money from my cousins Rick and Shantel and my God brother just to have money in my pocket. I wasn't able to help pay bills. I really was at a low space in my life. I didn't want to go out to find a job because I was waiting around for the union to call. I know it was a lot of pressure on my cousins to handle all the bills without my help.

Sometimes I wouldn't eat because I didn't have money and I didn't feel it was right to be eating up food I didn't help to buy. The only thing that took a lot of that stress away was basketball. I still played basketball every day. Where we stayed was about 5 miles from where I played basketball. I would walk to the gym, play 5 or more games and then walk back home. For those couple of hours I was in my safe place. This happened over the course of 8 months, until I was called for a job. It felt good to be able to help out my cousins with bills and food shopping. I was able to work for almost a year at this job until it was completed. This time didn't feel as bad because I was able to collect unemployment, so I had some money coming in to help pay bills. Still no matter what I was able to play basketball.

I learned a lot about basketball from my coaches, but I also learned a lot about life through this game of basketball. Wins and losses weren't the only things I took away from basketball. It taught me how to be determined, how to fight through adversities and how to stay positive in the mist of chaos. I owe the game of basketball my life. If it wasn't for the love of the game, I would probably be dead or in jail. No matter where life took me, basketball was always a factor.

During the time I was waiting for the union to call I got involved with some illegal activities. The unemployment was coming in but it wasn't enough. I had to bring in more money. I didn't want to go back to how I was when I barely ate food and had no money to do anything. So because of these activities I almost lost my life. I remember going to meet up with a young lady. I parked my car and went into the projects to get her. During this time I was always strapped, meaning I always had a gun on me. This particular time I left my gun in the car when I went into the building. As me and the young lady was coming down in the elevator, I had this strange feeling. We were in the elevator talking and when the door open there was a guy standing there with a gun pointed directly in my face. I couldn't do anything but say Jesus! It felt like my heart stopped beating. All I could think was I don't want to die. The young lady was scared and crying. I could barely hear her because I was hearing a voice in my head. As the guy was standing there, he didn't say a word. The voice in my head start to quote scripture. I don't know how I remembered this scripture. The scripture was Psalm 23:4. At that time I didn't know where it was located in the Bible. "As I walk through the valley of the shadow of death I will fear no evil for thou art with me". Again, I couldn't remember how I knew that or where I heard it. Now I believe it came from me being in church with my brother every Sunday. I never wanted to go so I sat up in the balcony with the other teens not really paying attention. But I know now that God was watching over me because the guy went to pull the trigger and the gun jammed. He cocked it back and pulled again and the gun still jammed. I couldn't believe what just happened, I just knew I was going to die. The guy ran off and the elevator door closed and I started crying and thanking God. God spared my life, but I didn't understand why at the time.

Time had passed, and I was still up to illegal activities. Even while I was doing illegal activities I still made time for basketball. I was bringing in good money and I loved it. Things were going well to me, I was able to pay bills, hang out and travel. During the time of me doing all these things I met this beautiful woman named Gwen that would later become my wife. This also changed my life. We met on a bus trip to the Poconos. A friend of mine worked with her in education and he invited me on the trip that she put together. After the trip we started dating and getting to know each other. I was still involved with my activities while I was dating her. I used to pick her up and take her daughter to school and her to work. Then I would pick them up after school and bring them home. So while I was in between union jobs and doing other things, during the day I would go outside on a nice day and play basketball with anyone who was out there. One morning when I dropped her off at work. Her assistant principal noticed me as I was driving away. Gwen called me and asked me would I be interested in working in education. Her principal had a friend that just opened a new school and was looking for staff. I told her I would think about it and let her know. When I returned home after dropping her off at work. My neighbor told me that detectives were looking for me. They told her they were looking for a guy that lived on the second floor in our two-family house. I started to worry, and I was on the lookout for anything out of order.

Then I thought is this a sign? When I picked Gwen up after work I told her I would go interview for the job. I went on the interview and got the job. Working in education wasn't something I thought I would end up doing. Working for the Board Of Education was a big deal where I came from. I just looked at it as a job and a way to make legit money. I didn't realize how working in a school would be something that I would fall in love with.

After getting this job, I was able to get a second job working at a recreation program. At this program I ran an afterschool program and an open gym for adults in the evenings. The open gym was the perfect situation for me. I was able to work and play basketball at the same time. During the summer I was able to run a basketball camp for the youth in my community. That summer made it clear that being a basketball coach was something I really wanted to be. After that summer I relocated to New Jersey with Gwen and our oldest daughter. I continued to work in education when I moved to Jersey. The first school district I worked at was Morningside Board of Education. I was there for five years. The way I built a relationship with a lot of the students was through basketball. I loved the game so much I would play with the students during their lunchtime and recess. Two months of working there I injured myself playing basketball with the students. I went to the doctor, and he said I tore my Achilles heel. He told me that I might need surgery if I wanted to play basketball ever again. The next day I was in surgery because I knew I couldn't go on forever without playing basketball again.

After the surgery and going through recovery was hard. The whole time my focus was on getting better so I could play basketball again. I went to rehab three times a week and whatever the doctor told me to do for home exercises I did. I pushed myself to get back on the court, you've would have thought I was an NBA player. I worked so hard in rehab my doctor rewarded me with lower-level seats to the Philadelphia 76ers game. The ironic thing is I tore my Achilles heel on October 31, 2001. Twenty-one years to the date that my mother passed away. I got injured in October and I was back on the basketball court in May. Those months I couldn't play basketball was hell. I felt depressed, frustrated, and useless. I didn't like that feeling so I worked so hard to get better. In June of 2002 I was back on the court full strength. I felt like I was back to myself.

During my time at Morningside I held afterschool basketball games for students who wanted to play. That was one of the ways I built relationships with students. I used that as a method to engage with students and at the same time mentor them. After being at Morningside for a few years, I left and took a job at a county technical high school for short as a Teacher's Aide. It took me no time to connect with the students. The connection was through the sport of basketball.

While working there I became friends with the head boys' basketball coach. From our conversations about basketball, he asked if I would like to volunteer to be an assistant coach for the program. I gladly accepted the offer and jumped right in coaching. I coached there for 5 years and I will say those were some of the best years of my life. After 5 years of volunteering, I applied for a fulltime assistant basketball coach position. I just knew I was a shoe in. I put in so much hard work over the last 5 years for free. Unfortunately, I didn't get the position and it broke my heart. For years after that I was very angry and frustrated that I didn't get the position. The crazy thing is during my time coaching there I was a major factor in leading the program to the most wins in school history at that time. For them to overlook me was wrong. At one point I lost my love for basketball so much that I wouldn't go to any games or have anything to do with the program. Not being able to coach basketball, I felt a void in my life like when my mom passed. I was just going through the motions of life. I never stopped playing basketball, but I felt like God spared my life for a reason but, I couldn't figure out why. That was until Gwen and I started an educational services company. Through the company we provided testing, tutoring, and counseling. The thing was those were the services she was able to do. I had to find a way to expand our services. We came up with a mentoring service to add to the company. In the past I worked as a mentor for another company. At first, I couldn't figure out how to structure the program, until Gwen asked me what I was passionate about. So, I designed a program around basketball. The program is called "Hope Through Hoops". I was teaching life skills to the kids through the game of basketball. Everyone that played sports knows how sports gave them experiences, and taught them lessons.

Through the grace of God in 2018 I was able to launch that program. I was contracted to run the program as an after school activity in the city of Camden, NJ for 3rd to 8th grade young men. The program was a success and I was contracted to return again the following year, but due to the Covid 19, in 2020 the program was cancelled. I was disappointed but one thing I learned over the years is what God has in store for you will be for you. Let me backtrack a little. The basketball program at the high school cleaned house and hired a whole new coaching staff. This was prior to me starting the Hope Through Hoops program. I only heard the name of one of the coaches before and that was the head coach. To be honest I didn't care for them because I was still angry for not getting the position.

One of the assistant coaches Antoine Miller, was also an Aide in the building. I had seen him around the building from time to time. We would speak in passing but that was it, until one of my co-workers invited Antoine to the area where we have lunch every day. Just from the conversations we all had during lunch I got to know Antoine. We became cool and built a friendship. We would have lunch together with other staff members where we talk about everything. We did talk about basketball during lunch, and he could see my passion and how I would lite up when we would have the conversations. He asked me why I stopped coaching and would I coach there again? I explained to him what happened and how it hurt me. As a result of the numerous conversations, I started to attend the boys' home games. Just standing there watching the games I felt the Holy Spirit saying you need to get back to what you love. I kept fighting it, making excuses for why it wouldn't work. Until about a couple of weeks after the basketball season Antoine mentioned that he was starting up an AAU basketball program. I asked him if he had a coaching staff and he said he didn't. I immediately volunteered to help, and he accepted. For some reason I felt this situation was different.

We launched the program" Camden Elite" in 2019 coaching 7th and 8th grade boys. We had a decent turn out for being a new program. Our program is built on teaching the game of basketball the correct way. One of the reasons why I wanted to coach with him is because I could feel his passion. He is just as passionate as I am about the game and our youth. The program is based around basketball but also preparing them for life. Our program like others came to a pause due to the pandemic in 2020. During that time Antoine left the school as an Aide but continued to be a part of the coaching staff. Even though we didn't work together we still had Camden Elite. AAU if you don't know can be very time consuming, so I was spending a lot of time away from home and my family. Gwen and I had a few disagreements over me spending time away not making any money from it. She would tell me I could have used that time to help bring more money into the house. I understood where she was coming from but I felt the Holy Spirit telling me to be faithful and trust in God. Once I found God and knew Him for myself, I stopped worrying about things. God always provided for me and my family. We never missed a meal or ever lacked the needs for anything. So I stayed committed to my passion. Talking to Antoine, he told me he got a head coaching job at a charter school in Camden. I didn't think anything of it at first, until he asked me if I would come be a part of his coaching staff and also recommended that I be hired as staff in the building. I was truly humbled and overwhelmed. I told my wife, and she was excited as well. My mind immediately wondered how this was going to work with me working at a different school. Not only working at another school, but it was also where our youngest daughter attends and I am her transportation to and from school. As excited as I was, I did have to have a talk with my family to see how this would all work out. The new position was a promotion and a nice raise in pay.

It took me a couple of weeks of thinking it over because I didn't want my daughter to transfer schools. She was doing well in school, and I didn't want to change her environment. Again, I have to say that God is a miracle worker. Based off the relationships I built over the years at the school, Ms. Tillman who lives near me volunteered to bring my daughter back and forth to school. When she said she would do that for me, I broke into tears with joy and gratefulness. It wasn't just her but my friend Ronn also volunteered. This made the decision so much easier. All my faith in God and knowing that he would give me the desires of my heart paid off. Not only had God blessed me with a great raise in salary but in the start of the 2023 high school basketball season, I would be sitting on the bench as an official high school assistant basketball coach and I'm looking forward to seeing what God has in store for me in the future as I continue my Love For The Game.

Rock Your Lane

Toni Moore

I was never comfortable living in the gross poverty I inherited from my ancestors. I needed something in my life that would help me upgrade from the station I was born into to the place I had hoped to be. I felt that somehow God accidentally put me with the wrong family. I had dreams, but we never had enough money to pay for any of my wants or most of my needs. I needed money to learn a skill, develop my talents, to grow above and beyond the Gross poverty line. Unfortunately, our money came through food stamps and monthly stipends, which never lasted past the twentieth day of any given month, but I refused to be stuck in the poverty I inherited.

As a child, I ran from the pain of poverty that hurt children's dreams, suppressed adults' natural inclination to pursue some level of happiness, and infiltrated the minds of criminals who preyed on those who prayed for a quick escape. I tried to hide the welts and bruises that resulted from frustrated means to compel certain behaviors and blind faith in a religion that caused many to acquiesce without inquiry. Unfortunately, I couldn't escape the fingers of men who unapologetically pried them into little girls with grown-up bodies.

I left the ghetto as soon as I could after graduating from the Milton Hershey School. Without knowing the full meaning of what I had been attracted to, I applied for and was accepted into the University of Pennsylvania. Getting into an Ivy League university was an easy task since I am naturally gifted with picking up information. However, staying there proved a challenging task since no one prepared me for the type of success that middle-class children educated in private schools were expected to achieve.

If I could, maybe I should become my mantra until I forgot that I was fearfully and wonderfully made to appreciate everything bottled within me. I no longer liked my hair, my clothes, my voice; myself so I tried to show up as someone else. I tried to do whatever I could to get others to see me, hear me and notice me by doing differently. Unfortunately, after so many do-overs, start overs, false starts, and restarts, I no longer liked who I absentmindedly allowed myself to become. Something within me spewed out of control. You see, I tried to get in and fit in so that others didn't notice my faults and deficiencies. But even though I tried to be who others wanted me to become, it wasn't good enough for them. Rejection after rejection after rejection, I tried so much so that I stopped trying to appease and just allowed myself to go dark.

And I went full out. I began spewing venom and allowing hatred to fester in me. I was a pretty face but a pretty mess. During that time of darkness, I lost long-time friends, went through lovers, lost my job, and feverishly avoided mirrors because I couldn't stand who I had allowed myself to become—I couldn't function without a man or alcohol to help me forget. I had reached a new level of brokenness wherein all that I knew myself to be was removed. I felt so rejected that I wanted to end it all. But my Pentecostal upbringing eliminated any options of doing wrong with my body. Instead, I prayed to see another side of heaven. Loneliness and inherited depression will skew one's perception so much so that you only see problems, pain, confusion, chaos, and negativity. In my distress, I asked for an intervention to remove my unhappiness. When all hope of having, doing, and being more seemed like a foolish girl's desperate fantasy, I cried out and asked for an illness that would wipe me out. And that's when I had an encounter with the Holy One. Some would call it a Divine Intervention, others a Holy Encounter, whatever name it is referred to, I needed it.

One day while I was sleeping, I had a dream wherein my spirit travailed for me. My spirit wept, wailed, and prayed throughout the night because it wanted to live. But my soul was persuaded that I was unworthy. I had become judge, jury, and warden without so much allowing grace to speak up or advocate for my worthiness. As I slept, I wept in my sleep. I tossed, turned, and cried in my sleep. The life story was on trial and my soul and spirit were on opposite sides. While I slept and wept, my spirit literally prayed that I could appreciate my significance, potential, and possibilities. The prayer that crept from deep down in the seat of my spirit was a soul-stirring cry for help. It was what was needed to free my spirit and release my soul from living beneath who God planned and purposed me to be.

That one prayer was more than enough to awaken my hopes, dreams, and possibilities. While going through the fire, I realized that breakdowns help us appreciate the power within us to break through. But for pain, I would have never known the resilience within me to resist being a mere status quo of society. But for seeking God's help to erase me from the pain that I knew, I would have never been a beneficiary of Divine Intervention. But for my spirit crying out in anguish, I don't know where my dark soul would have been. Thankfully, when I woke up, I was weepy, tearful, and driven to attend church.

I woke up to attend a Sunday morning church service. I didn't know where I was going, I didn't have church clothes, nor did I know anyone at the church. But I went to the church that happened to be seven blocks away. Once I realized through hearing the Word of God that I was entitled to love, worthy of happiness, and more than enough to live my dreams, I began setting boundaries. I began making demands on myself, and I began setting the intention to become the woman of my dreams.

One way or another, we have all experienced some level of God's grace, especially when you are experiencing doubt, fear, hate, and extreme fatigue after trying to achieve a seemingly unreachable goal. What I've learned in my quest to become more than a statistic in urban society, old ways won't open new doors. So instead of getting caught up scratching and surviving, find something to thrive in. When you grow through what you go through, you are less likely to give away soulful keepsakes that empowered you to appreciate that you can live, love, and become who you choose to be. Each day is much like a blank slate, an empty page in a book, a blank canvas waiting for you to think, speak and do something that affects what's next. So never express what you don't want to see. Never get so focused on the things you hate. Nor get stuck in mediocrity, defeat, or the cult of sameness. Instead, you must continually seek, know, and do whatever it takes to manifest what God spoke over you. The same way we hurt ourselves, we can help ourselves. Whether dealing with family, lovers, or church hurt, you have the power to heal yourself.

To empower your desires, here are three things I learned to do that may be helpful to you. First, you must harness your power to become the wo/man of your dreams. It took me a long time to fully appreciate that I already am who I wanted to be. But now that I know better, I realize that no one can do for us what we're supposed to do for ourselves. From losing weight to saving money for retirement, you must do whatever it takes to turn your dream into a reality. When your job isn't working for you, find a way to find a job that fulfills you. Similarly, if you want to write a book, rebrand yourself, or even become a better version of yourself, just do it. Learn my lesson, don't wait for life to manifest greater for you, manifest greatness from you. Seek God's wisdom, guidance, grace, favor, and whispers that will lead you and guide you to spaces and places that empower you to become a more better you.

Second, you must write your vision of success. Whether you want to share meaningful marriage vows, run a more profitable business, or want to become a healthier version of yourself, you must write your vision. You don't have to be formal about writing your vision. You can write a note to yourself, a letter to your future self, or even write out a one-page vision statement. Study after study has shown the magic in writing your vision. Even the Bible reminds us of the importance of writing our vision and making it plain so that any reader can pick up and run with it. In writing my own vision of success, I empowered myself to have more, do more, and be more because I made my words matter to me. I believe the same can happen to you too!

Thirdly, you must become intentional about showing up for what you want. Many of us absently speak about what we don't want because that's what we learned to do. Perhaps you were told to wait your turn or to stop asking and just be satisfied. However, after continually succeeding in one small feat after another, I'm a true believer that you must be intentional in executing your goals. Take a moment within each day to appreciate who you are and empower your footsteps by affirming who God created you to be. When you get to a place where you want to take your life back, begin thinking about who you are, where you have been, and the keepsakes you learned through your journey of becoming. Never stop believing in yourself because you'll stop becoming who you're meant to be once you do. Never stop speaking your dreams because once you do you won't fulfill a greater destiny. And whatever you do, never stop pushing past the obstacles because once you do, you'll miss out on the opportunities to transform yourself into who God planned, purposed, and preordained you to be. You owe yourself to go through and grow through the fire so that you can become a reflection of God's desires.

Toni Moore, Esquire, is an Intellectual Property Attorney and Business Development Strategist with more than twenty years of business structuring, real estate, asset protection and estate planning experience. Throughout her career as a business lawyer, Toni has created companies, restructured companies, developed Strategic Plans, and assessed Corporate Compliance Plans, Policies and Procedures to ensure compliance with applicable rules and regulations. Toni has been doing whatever she can to empower others to make change possible in life and business throughout her professional career.

God, Help Me to be Manle

Michael Hunt

I can remember being a teenager having vivid dreams about how my life would turn out. I would wake up from those dreams looking forward to the unknown future that would have set me ablaze by my tenacity and uncompromising will. I vividly remember in one dream visions that set me on a path that would dictate who I am supposed to be with for the rest of my life. She would be the companion that I could talk to for hours about serious and silly ", along with trusting her with my innermost secret thoughts. I truly felt I found that person in my younger teenage years and her presence hit me an uppercut in the gut. I could hear a voice in my soul speaking to me at the sight of the girl saying, "This is going to be your wife, this is the woman you're going to spend the rest of your life with". At first sight of her, she was amazing, she had an illuminating smile, chocolate brown skin, nice hairstyle, especially for the 90s, (cause we all wish we could take back some of the trends or styles in that era). Not to mention she had "BODY", She was an around the way Filet, she was a tender Roney, she was a Chocolate deluxe! She was everything a young teenager could want, but what am I supposed to do with all these feelings at this time, is this even possible to have truth at the age of 13, and it could be reality? This vision or dream would start me on the path to adulthood that would and continues to be the most difficult and purposeful vision of my life. At that time there were plenty of men in my life that I could mirror or shadow that could help me with this prophecy that could keep me on the straight path so I could have the goal of being the man, husband, and father. I was eagerly looking for examples of good men in my life since my father passed when I was 9, and deep-down loneliness was an overwhelming feeling that felt like a weighted blanket of depression. My teenage years, from 13 to 19, the age I graduated, shaped many of my best and worst qualities, some to this very day. I grew up in a Pentecostal church, along with a very vast church community, where you spent your Sundays going to 8 am service, then Sunday school at 9:30, then to 11 am Sunday service, and if you didn't get a word from those you had Sunday night service at 7 pm, in essence, you spent all day in church. Most of my examples of manhood for me came from the church community. The church community is imperfect however it can be the greatest example of the process of perfection at the same time. That imperfection can be the byproduct of negative behavior and be the catalyst that drives to bad decisions and an unfulfilling life if you're not doing a daily inventory of the perpetual sin you fight, as well as overcoming your sinful nature. In my life, I've had male influencers, from childhood pastors to sports coaches, to family members that showed me what being a good husband, father, and overall man should be, however, most of these men suffered from not being able to express their feelings about the pitfalls and pains that come with the titles that they have. This was my main struggle. I did not have men in my life to show me how to deal with feelings of doubt, depression, frustration, anger, wrath, procrastination, sadness, and sexual desires. The management of how to deal with these feelings is my testimony through the fire. My experience of being a man has been rather entertaining. If you were to ask any man, how would he describe manhood you would get a different answer depending on the type of man you ask. My experience isn't and shouldn't be the overall definitive description of what a man should be, but the emotions that I hope to display in this chapter could shed some light on the ability of feelings a man would have and hopes to overcome. Through the eyes of the elders and men of my age, men are to be emotionless, cold, rigid, and almost robotic. We are too quick to shut down, or be short of words, if you cry you are weak, or not worthy of the man title. The fire was I did not have the Godly role models to show me how to handle my feelings through healthy practices, and it reared its ugly head when it came to how men approached their marriages and families. I'm not trying to say I'm a victim, and that all my sins and shortcomings were because of someone else, I'm saying that these influences left such an impact, that fed my sinful ways to breed practices that left me in a state that took time and prayer, while seeking true Godly counsel, as well as diligently seeking positive male examples.

Becoming a Husband

With the back story laid out, you could imagine my joy and satisfaction when that day came for my bride and me to become one in our union. That perfect day couldn't come soon enough, the planning, preparation, and color layouts that I had no idea even existed, all became worth it when I saw my wife walking down the aisle. Proverbs 18:22 says" He who finds a wife finds a good thing and obtains favor from the Lord". During the whole ceremony, I truly felt favored, and during the honeymoon, I realized she is truly a good thing. Once the honeymoon was over, then began the embarkation of the growing phase that involved situations that even though I knew how to start the process, I learned that the previously divulged information from past male experiences was obsolete at best. Externally while keeping a reserved and composed demeanor, I felt a bigger feeling of frustration, and anger germinating within, gradually growing with every personal deflection, while remembering the past advice from my peers, and friends that were married. That practice left me in a state of being where I felt emotionally detached, with the occasional Anger missile that would be directed toward the foundation blocks of my marriage. Matthew 5:37 says, "But let your 'Yes' be 'Yes,' and your 'No,' 'No' for whatever is more than these is from the evil one. Meaning not make special vows, or sentiments and not to swear falsely but perform your oaths to perform to the Lord. Personally, I was in a place where I was making promises I had zero intentions of keeping. My dreams and aspirations in the relationship were unfulfilled and all that was needed was a cataclysmic event that could test a marriage. That event was two miscarriages. I had no idea how to handle this, and the situation left me in a state where I tried to communicate with my wife however, the current practice of periodically being detached, or coasting under the radar of conflict just to keep peace came to a head. Did I have valid reasons for my feelings, ABSOLUTELY! Is it healthy for me to think how something like this happened to a couple that was full of love, OF COURSE! Subsequently, since a constant diet of communication during times of conflict was to deflect, stay under the radar, or fire an emotional missile were go-to weapons in warfare of arguments, this put my relationship in the fire!

The Greasy Truth

I love this part of the testimony, and if you know me you will understand. God is so merciful and graceful. Scripture talks about how the Lord will give you a way of escape in a situation in our lives as long, as we are aware of his omnipresence. He will give you the ability to bear whatever temptation that wants to overtake you (I COR 10:13). Meaning, that we must be conscious of our sinful nature, or flaws we have for us to walk righteously the path of holiness and success. In 2013, post-miscarriage I felt my wife was reaching a successful point in her life where it seemed like in my point of view, she was blazing a trail. Her hesitancy toward school transformed to where she thrived scholastically. Along with pursuing education, she started a budding career with being an event coordinator. I was proud of her success and triumphs; however, I couldn't deny what my feelings were. Howbeit proud along with her progression, feeling a bit jealous of the success being achieved. The dreams and closeness to the Lord were gone, it felt like he closed his ear to me. I gained over 40 pounds, the heaviest I've ever become. There was an opportunity for employment in the ministry that if accepted would potentially be a six-figure salary with benefits. The interview was going to be intense, but this could be the opportunity to grow and possibly get rid of the stagnancy I felt spiritually, and financially. Only a crazy person would turn this downright. When I presented this offer to my wife, with a slight pause in her voice she told me "The greasy truth". She told me that I was not ready for ministry, she told me if I wasn't properly leading in my home how could I lead a people group. She would prefer the reality of me staying in a position where I'm accumulating up to 75 hours of work in a week, with the potential of a 3rd job looming barely being home, than for me to take this position. As much as I wanted to be angry at her opinion, she was right. At that time if I could be honest, I was far from the man I envisioned previously in this testimony. Through my admission I allowed myself to fall so far that the things I found joy in were no longer a refuge from the stresses of life, the plan of purpose for my life was discarded for the need to make a quick buck. Instead of seeking the Lord in everything that I would do, I trusted in my own logic which further fed the inward insecurities, doubt, and depression. The lust of the flesh began to be untamed. Instead of my wife feeling loved, she later told me, it led to her feeling like a piece of meat, or just a booty call.

The Manle Change

I felt the fall from grace. The only thing I could do in the middle of the night in March 2013, was pray to the Lord God this prayer. I asked The Lord to show me everything that I'm doing wrong so I won't ever feel this feeling again of being alone and without him, then BOOM! He showed me every sin, every internal feeling that I swept under the rug, the inexcusable behavior of miscommunication that hindered me from expressing my true feelings in every relationship I had qualms with. The purpose and plan for building a unique ministry where I would thrive, it was the very vision that was shown during the engagement planning for marriage. The Lord also showed me that we would have a child organically without IVF treatment. Most of all I would lead my house as the Man God called me to be and garner the respect that was missing at the time. Righteousness starts immediately after the confession and must have a plan of attack to remain set apart. First, I had to start with Proverbs 9:10," The fear of the Lord is the beginning of wisdom, and the knowledge of the Holy One is understanding." Once When I had a renewed understanding of the ways of the Lord, I applied His wisdom to everything. I did an eternal cleanup in my mind and started doing basic exercises to express my need to communicate. One Ph.D. professor held a conference on being a better communicator in one's relationship that one should communicate for understanding. This professor also said that these conferences showed the following in attendance 91% women and only 9% men. Information like this made my wife and I start a feelings challenge. It was over a hundred words that we had to express our feelings. This changed my life, it made me center my mind from the insecurity of communicating, to blossom into an interaction machine. My wife will say that I'm the leader of this action, I will try to do a weekly inventory of our relationship to breed healthy discussion about, insecurities, wants, needs, finances, and sex. This led me to build a space of intimacy that encouraged healthy talk about our sexual experience that was hindered. I Peter 3:7 says, "Husbands, likewise, dwell with them with understanding, giving honor to the wife, as to the weaker vessel, and as being heirs together of the grace of life, that your prayers may not be hindered." This is my life scripture that the Lord showed as an insurance policy to all husbands not honoring this scripture toward their wives. God almighty will literally delay or hinder your prayers if we as husbands do not give honor to our wives. We must learn not to deflect or disengage and keep our behinds home in the moment with our Covenant keeper. Before marriage, I was a whore, which led to vivid pictures of past partners that mentally brought comparison to my wife, and that mental Adultery had to stop! 2 Cor. 10: 3- 6 says, "For though we walk in the flesh, we do not war according to the flesh. For the weapons of our warfare are not carnal but mighty in God for pulling down strongholds, casting down arguments and everything that exalts itself against the knowledge of God, bringing every thought into captivity to the obedience of Christ, (Very important is verse 6) And being ready to punish all disobedience when your obedience is fulfilled. Keep in mind the devil is not mentioned, this is an eternal battle that could only be won with the missile of God's word. This Truth led me to take my holiness seriously, I encourage anyone married to make, build, and prioritize your spouse to be your accountability partner. This will encourage a deeper marriage cause now you'll be able to meet the need for insecurity in your marriage, where feelings of loneliness, lust, and anger can be met with love and understanding, while you're going through the fire. Lastly, it made me change my social media to Manle Mike, the "E" standing for supplying the emotional content that a man truly owns. If a man can express a cover 0 blitz in football, or explain a high screen in roll, in basketball he can learn to express love and what he needs in a relationship.

In Closing

My ministry was birthed through the fire. The Lord fashioned me to be an example that you can concur and eradicate your sinful nature. Do I make mistakes? Yes. Do I still get on my wife's nerves? Of course, but now she knows my heart and can honor my position in the home. I'm the leader in my home, not by force or by dictatorship, but according to Ephesians 5: 22-29. Mainly the verse overlooked is 29, "For no one ever hates his own flesh, but nourishes and cherishes it, just as the Lord does the Church." To any man reading this, I pray that you find value in these words nourish and cherish, you have the power in you to perform those words, I Love You, and that's coming from a strong Manle place inside.

Faith through Adversity

Tiffany D Bell

It was an early Thursday morning. My husband, Kenneth, was sitting on the side of the bed telling me softly that it was time to wake up. He was already dressed. I had gotten to bed a little later than usual the night before and really wanted to continue to sleep.

"Tiff," he said, "You've got to get going. You are going to be late to work." I slowly came to my senses. I looked up at him as he smiled and bent over to kiss my forehead.

I met Ken after his car flipped while on a road trip to his hometown near Myrtle Beach, South Carolina. His family had agreed to meet there for Thanksgiving. It was almost love at first sight. We hit it off instantly. Within two weeks, he told me that he knew that he was going to marry me. Five months later, we tied the knot! He was the love of my life.

Even after I had fully awakened, I was incredibly stressed that morning. I felt terribly uneasy. I did not really know why though. I also did not have time to think much about it. I hurriedly dressed for work. I did not allow myself to acknowledge it. Our regular routine was that Ken would take the kids to school on his way into his job. After getting dressed, I gathered my things and headed out the door. I hesitated for a moment.

I thought, "Should I kiss Ken good-bye or just get on the road?" I cannot remember what I decided.

Once I arrived at work, I felt as if I should give Ken a call.

"Why?" I wondered. It just did not make sense. I called him a few times. No answer.

About 10:00 A.M. I sent him a text that said, "I love you." Still, the feeling would not go away. By 2:00 P.M. that day, I could not take it anymore. I had a powerful urge to be near Ken. It was all that I could think about.

My boss let me leave early. It was nearly 2:30.

I did not know where to head. I just knew that I needed to find him. I drove over a block near the mall and picked up my phone to give him a call again. This time, a woman answered. That had never happened before. I identified myself to her and asked for Ken. She did not answer me.

But, I did hear her say, "Doctor, this is his wife."

Shortly after, the doctor began to speak.

"Ma'am, I am an ER doctor with Biloxi Regional Medical Center. Your husband has had an accident." I immediately asked if he was alright. After three times of asking him, he finally said that my family and I should come to the hospital to say our good-byes.

Never in a million years did I see that coming. Ken was only 34 years old. He was young, vibrant, wise, loving, and kind. He was the kind of guy that people were drawn to. He accepted everyone. Ken believed strongly in community and taking care of the needs of family, friends, and strangers alike.

He loved being a father. Ken knew that since age five, that he wanted to be a dad. He also had an excellent relationship with his mom. He cherished her and wanted to take care of her as she entered retirement age. We thought that we would grow old together. We were supposed to be that nearly ninety-year-old couple holding hands on an evening stroll.

When I ended the call with the doctor, I yelled at God.

I said, "This is not what you promised. This is not a part of the plan!"

My entire future was lost. How was I going to take care of two boys? I lived 700 miles away from my family. His family lived even farther away. What was I going to do?

I grew quiet. I sat for several minutes, trying to formulate a plan. I had to tell my kids. How was I going to tell his mom? The doctor wanted me to come and identify his body. I knew that that was not going to happen.

If I did not know anything else, I knew that I would preserve my last memory of him. I was going to remember how helpful he was as we worked to get the boys ready for school that morning. I would remember hearing him singing in the shower.

What was I supposed to do about his business? His equipment? The rental houses? All of that would need to be taken care of. It was all so much to deal with.

At this point, I began to address the Lord again. I also knew that my attitude needed an adjustment. I remember telling Him that if this were how things would be, He was responsible for making sure that everything the boys and I needed would be taken care of. It was too much for me to handle. I honestly felt that He was obligated to take care of us.

And, of course, He did.

I quickly learned that I was not alone in my grief. Immediately, people poured in from all around to help us. Ken was well known among his military and church family. So many blessings came our way, I could hardly keep up. We were inundated with support from friends and family. Not a single thing went undone that year. The comfort and love that we were shown made a difference in my heart. Slowly I began to move forward in and what it meant to live a life without him.

My progress was slow at first though. I learned a lot about myself in Ken's death. I realized that I had lived a self-focused life. I loved God, but I cannot say that I really loved my neighbor. Ken tried teaching me small lessons over the years about love... how to communicate it, how to receive it, and how to reciprocate it. It was not until he died that the lessons began to sink in.

I began to want to do more with my life and to do more for my community. But I was afraid. I really did not know where to start or really what it meant to be more, do more, or give more. I had spent so many years living to survive. I did not know what it really meant to thrive.

If you consider having a lot of possessions thriving, then yes, we were thriving. We owned several vehicles, houses, and a business. But I did not know the real *Tiffany*. Who was I outside of the kids and Ken? I was a timid girl that was filled with fear and plagued by insecurity. What was I supposed to do to move forward? Could I do something more with my life? And if so, how? Where would I start? It was time to develop a life that did not revolve solely around me.

The Lord began directing me on how to create a new life for myself and the boys. I started by re-evaluating our lifestyle and some of the choices that Ken and I had made. I discovered that I was living a comfortable life but was not truly fulfilled. I began to volunteer with my local church and community organizations, and I soon realized that I wanted to do more.

But before I could begin to volunteer more, I needed to do something about the fear and insecurity that had always been present in my life. I started by developing better study habits surrounding God's word. I began to journal more frequently and I identified lies that I had believed all of my life. I learned how to deal with my feelings. I also surrounded myself with people that were positive and supportive.

I think that one of the most effective things that I did regularly was to laugh. I laughed a lot! I would watch funny movies, read funny books and just generally find things to make me happy. It was an intentional effort to replace sadness with happiness.

Ken was always laughing. He was pretty funny and he had a way to make people laugh naturally. He would have wanted the boys and me to continue laughing. He would not want us to become buried in grief.

Slowly but surely, I started to develop a new life for myself. It was not an easy process, but it was worth it. I began to see that I could do more than just survive; I could thrive. The Lord showed me that He is always with me and that He will never leave me. He also gave me the courage to face my fears and to do something more with my life.

There is hope for those who are grieving. If you have lost a loved one, know that you are not alone in your grief. There are people who care about you and want to help you through this difficult time. Lean on your friends and family for support, and seek out professional help if needed. Remember that the Lord is with you and will not leave you.

This was a new journey for me, but it was one that I needed to take if I wanted to move forward in life. Widowhood had presented some unique challenges, but I refused to let them defeat me. With the help of God, family, and friends, I was able to survive my husband's death and create a new life for myself and my boys and I am still thriving today.

When someone we love dies, it feels like our world has come to an end. We are left feeling confused, hurt, and alone. For many widows, coping with the death of a spouse can be one of the most difficult things they ever face in their lives. As I grew stronger, I was able to do more things that helped me move forward in my life.

The most important thing that I did was to surround myself with a support system of family and friends. These people helped me through the tough times and celebrated with me during the good times.

Mourning the death of a spouse is one of the most difficult things a person can go through. But with God's help, you can get through it. You will have hard days and good days, but know that you are not alone. Lean on your support system and allow yourself to heal in your own time. Remember, you are strong and you can do this!

When I look back on that year, I see how much we all changed. The boys were forced to grow up quickly and learn how to live without their dad. They had to learn how to lean into God and find Him in the midst of their pain.

I had to learn how to mourn with uncommon courage.

It has now been over 15 years since Ken died. We still miss him every day, but we have learned to live life without him in it. We have found ways to honor him and keep his memory alive. Each of us has found our own way of thriving in spite of our grief.

Grief is a difficult journey, but it is not a journey that we have to take alone. We have the support of a loving God and community who wants to see us succeed. With their help, we can move forward with uncommon courage. That is how this chapter came to be. I am still on that journey. It is one that I never imagined taking, but it is a beautiful journey nonetheless.

As I sit down to write this, I am reminded of a conversation that Ken and I had shortly before he died. We were talking about heaven and he said to me, "Tiffany, when I get to heaven, the first thing I am going to do is run and give God a big hug." One of his favorite songs was "I Can Only Imagine" by MercyMe.

I am not the same woman that I was when Ken died. I am stronger, braver and more confident. And while my pain will always be there, it does not consume me like it once did. Grief is a process and it takes time, but eventually the sadness will give way to happiness again – a happiness that is found in knowing that Ken is now with the Lord and that one day we will be reunited.

I am so grateful that I know he is there waiting for me with open arms. And until I get there, I will continue to honor his life and legacy with uncommon courage. My journey is one of grief, love, and redemption, and it is a testament to the power of the human spirit. In the face of overwhelming tragedy, I have found the courage to carry on and to thrive.

In conclusion, I encourage you to do the same. Lean on God, family, and friends during this difficult time and allow yourself to heal in your own way. You are strong and you can do this!

AB+

_____

Pastor Jimmy Lindsay

Recently I donated Plasma and received my blood donor card in the mail that showed my blood type. The card said I was AB+ and me not knowing what that means, I decided to look that up and research what AB+ means. Much to my surprise I found some things that kind of put some other things into perspective. The first thing that I found out is that AB+ blood type is rare, that only 2% of donors are AB+. The 2nd thing I found out is that AB+ blood types CAN receive blood from ANYONE, and the 3rd thing that I found out was that AB+ blood types can ONLY give to other AB+ blood types despite being able to receive from any other blood type.

This journey started for me on October 18th 1973 at Albert Einstein Medical Center in Philadelphia, PA. At the time I was my mother's 3rd child and my father's 1st child. I was born into a large family, where my mother was 1 of 7, but my mother unable to care for child number 3, decided to put "James Murphy" up for adoption, against the birth fathers will, just days into being born. It was written to me that my mother had to go through a process to keep parental rights after my birth, but because of not fulfilling certain obligations her parental rights were revoked and that would be the very last time seeing either of my birth parents. What am I to do with this major disruption in my life that turned out to be very traumatic? Life was about to take a turn that I didn't ask for, nor did I deserve.

So here I am, days old and in the State of Pennsylvania "System" as a ward of the state for the first 3 years of my life. I was immediately placed into foster care and placed in several homes. I do not have much recollection about these homes but I was told that I had to be snatched from one of the homes because I was being "abused" in some way that I do not know of. The last foster home that I was in for a long time, had to give me up because they were up in age and realized they couldn't take care of such a young child, and the story is told that I was devastated. Not even 3 years old and traumatized all over again.

Sometime after turning 3 in October of 1976 a married couple in their mid-30's and mid-40's from a small town in New Jersey called Palmyra came across the Tacony Palmyra bridge to the Children's Aid Society of PA wanting to adopt a child. According to my mom, when my dad saw me he said that's my son and Jimmy C. Lindsay was birthed. Although they know the broken areas in this little boy's life that needed attention and mending, did they know the trauma that had already begun to shape this little boy?

Let me share with you some of the broken pieces that made up this little incomplete boy Jimmy. The meaning of the name Jimmy in Dictionary.com is someone or something taking the place of another, as through force, scheming, strategy, or the like. In the Bible Saint James, of course, was one of Jesus' 12 apostles, and the meaning was "supplanter" or "replacer." It's derived from the Latin Jacomus which also means "may God protect." So when my name was given to me, whether it was James Murphy or Jimmy Lindsay, I was born to take the place of another and God was protecting me.

This vessel that looked put together by the average eye, but thru the Spiritual eye I was just a vessel that was broken and put back together and held with something that could not withstand the pressure on the inside......WALK WITH ME thru this trauma.

At an early age I knew that I was adopted and my mother's sister also adopted a son who is about three years older than me. For some reason he and I were always very close, I spent the night over there often, I helped him deliver his papers, he would come and pick me up, and when it came time for me to drive I even bought his first car from him, a 1978 Pontiac Firebird. We had this connection that I paid no attention to but looking back I understand that this AB+ could only pour into another AB+, or someone similar. Remember AB+ can only give to other AB+ individuals, so everything that I did and said was being poured into him and only he could receive it.

As time passed I realized that I had these learned behaviors, where did I get them from? All these learned and unlearned behaviors that I developed going from home to home. I am a broken vessel, and one of my broken pieces is "lack of communication". I often feel that what I have to say does not matter. I mean if it mattered, then my biological mother would have interpreted my crying and listened to me. I was telling her, like any child, that I NEED YOU. With every push as I was being birthed, and every tear that I cried when I made my grand entrance into this world I was saying I NEED YOU. I guess you couldn't hear me, I guess, you weren't listening and decided to give up the most precious GOD given gift. So that is where it started, when my emotions were muted, my tongue was locked and I had nothing else to say. I developed these waves of emotions and did not know how to express it, how does a child begin to speak? How does this little boy grow into a man and still not know how to express himself? Where do these pent up emotions go? NOWHERE... When I was a teenager I got into some trouble and my mom decided to get me therapy. The one thing that the therapist said to me that stuck in my head was that "One day Jimmy was going to explode and someone was going to get hurt". All because of my lack of communication. I learned to hold it all in and eternalize the emotions that came with it. I often say that I am dial up not high speed...I need time to think, process and connect. I developed these folders in my mind, and all that I WANT to say but don't say is stored in these "folders". They are to be used later or archived to never be seen, but sometimes that folder runs out of storage and a few times I found myself EXPLODING and not knowing why. My storage was full and I had to delete some stuff to make room for some other stuff and the only way I could delete it is was by blowing up about something that had nothing to do with WHY , just so this non communicator can get out some stuff that he didn't know how to express. I developed really bad headaches because of the pressure, nothing could ease it. I developed anxiety and my thoughts kept me from resting when I was asleep. I didn't ask for this, I'm just a kid, what am I to do? I know what I'll do, I'll become a great listener. I'll create another folder and name it "NO JUDGEMENTS". I'll make myself available to listen to people as they pour out their fears, shortcomings, heartaches and whatever else they need to get off their chest. They could pour into me, but I would never pour into them. AB+, I can receive from ANYONE but I can NOT reciprocate to everyone. So ill mask my lack of communication by mastering the art of listening, I mean that can work for me right? It would surely keep people AROUND and they would not leave me. WRONG, that created an even stronger thinking that what I have to say isn't as important as what I need to hear or what you need to say. Mind you, I didn't say that it caused me stress or emotional problems, it didn't keep me awake at night, WHY IS THAT?

It's because another piece that was broken was my EMOTIONS. I developed an "I don't care attitude". I had to protect my emotions, I had to guard myself, I was hurt by the one that gave birth to me and for the next 3 years the constant in and out from one place to another coupled with abuse forced me to be emotionally distant, so that I wouldn't get hurt. If I did get hurt then I would have to find a way to hurt you back. You can't just hurt me and get away with it. My emotions were wrecked, bad things didn't seem to affect me like they did others, and I didn't know how to deal with emotions when I experienced them. My instant reaction was to find the problem and see how I could fix it. This was my cover up for being so emotionless, I disguise my lack of emotion with "fixing". So I've covered up my lack of communication by being a great listener, and now I have to master "fixing" to cover my lack of emotions. I learned to not put my heart into much because I didn't want to get hurt. I didn't want to get close to anyone, I just wanted to be with me, because I would not hurt myself. I could trust me with me, but I could not trust you with me. I desperately needed someone to accept and validate my feelings. Those feelings of doubt, loneliness, disappointment, abandonment did not have an outlet because of my lack of communicating and lack of emotions. On the flip side of that I am very empathetic towards what others are experiencing or going thru, mainly because I want to help you to not feel like me. Suddenly the question becomes: how can I make you happy? What did I do wrong? How can I make it better? Wait a minute, I'm the one that's hurt, not you. Wait a minute Jimmy, don't get emotional, it's just you. You'll be ok, TRUST me.

This leads me to another piece that was broken called TRUST, because of this trauma I lacked trust. I'm just a baby, I can't take care of myself, I didn't ask to be here, but all life is a gift from GOD right? If I'm a gift then why didn't you take the time to unwrap me and put me together? Why did you abandon me? I'm trusting you will take care of me and not abandon me. My life is in your hands, I'm depending on you to give me all that I need to be great, all that I need to survive. We have bonded in the womb, I know your voice, so why have you done this to me? The line of trust has been broken. Because of you the abuse and neglect began. My trust in people is shattered before it even really began. You haven't been listening to me, I can't trust you. You left me when I needed you the most, I can't trust you. You say you love me then you break my heart, I can't trust you. Now anybody I meet that happens to resemble any of these things I automatically put them in that folder labeled "distrust". Behind this smile and chubby cheeks is a story of pain from a child whose basic needs were not met. I don't understand why the very people that should have loved me didn't. My mom has a picture of me sitting on my big wheel right in front of the steps at the front door to our house and mom tells the story that whenever she would put me out the house and on my big wheel she would try to get me to ride up and down the sidewalk, but I wouldn't move. She didn't understand why, I wouldn't say anything, I would just sit there. What mom didn't know is that I was scared that if I rode down this sidewalk that she wouldn't be there when I got back. Somehow she would leave me like everyone else that I loved. I didn't trust she would be there. As I am writing this I am 48 years old and my dad passed away 3 weeks ago at the age of 91, and that 3 year old little boy showed his face in this 48 year old grown man. I've never felt these emotions before, I wailed and cried like I had never done before over anyone or anything. Where are these emotions coming from? Then I told my wife that I had no idea how I was going to be able to move on, my heart was broken. Now I'm reliving these feelings of abandonment and asking myself why would he leave me like that? I'm still that little boy sitting on his big wheel scared that you won't be there when I get back. These are the long term effects of trauma that weren't properly addressed.

So the question that begs to be answered is after all this how did you even begin to overcome all of this? The answer is... I HAVEN'T... but there have been some things that have helped me to deal with this trauma and deal with it head on. I know it sounds cliché but the greatest thing my mom could have done for that broken 3 year old boy was take him to church. Why you ask, because church gave me something to attach to that was not going anywhere. So remember, I didn't want to leave for fear of being left, so church gave me the ability to attach myself to something that would always be constant. As a result of that I began to immerse myself and put my ALL into church, and before you know it I had a love affair with church and GOD. I learned about all aspects of the church. I was involved in all events that the Black Baptist Church had to offer. I was in the choir, Sunday school, Bible study, the State and National Associations, I was even the sexton at my church. This was really my turning point because the first thing I was exposed to as my mom and dad's son was church where I began to learn about forgiveness, that there's someone greater than me that is looking out for me, that this trauma did not have to define me, and that I had to dig deeper to find who I really am. What is my purpose? Can I really be someone of influence? Could I actually be a husband and an effective father someday? Even though this happened after my adoption I say it's the most important part because it really is the nucleus of everything. When we can realize that GOD controls everything and knows everything you begin to see the hand of GOD moving when you didn't even know who GOD was. Nothing happens by chance, it may not feel good, it may not sound good but on the other side of "through" you'll be able to look back and see how you've just been on the potter's wheel being shaped and molded, and if there was a flaw the potter just had to put you back in the fire for a little while just so the potter can correct what was flawed. This way when the enemy does try to break you, you can withstand the heat. Little did I know that some years later that I would help three families as they prepared to adopt and through those crucial times in those kids' lives. So GOD has a funny way of turning our pressure into progress and our fire into fight.

Right next to my faith is family. Family is what showed me who I am and what I want. My adopted mother completed high school, took some college courses and worked very hard and retired from FORD Motor Credit. Whereas my dad was 9 years older than my mother, had a 7th grade education, was in the Korean War, and retired as a construction worker with a modest income. These two totally opposite people showed me who I was and what I wanted in life. I never wanted for anything, and Christmas was an unbelievable sight in and outside my house. So coming from nothing, no family, no guidance and no sense of being; to celebrating me every October 18th and then receiving all these missing pieces to my puzzle played a major role in the shifting of my development and mindset. I focused on family so much that when the family began to separate and do their own thing, I took it upon myself to do what I could in order to keep certain traditions in tack. I developed this love of the idea of family so much that my wife and I had our first child 1 month before our 1 year anniversary. The people I call family has taken this stranger in and made him son, cousin, nephew...etc., It was the greatest feeling ever, how could anyone ever be without family. How could a parent purposely take that away from their child before it even starts? Little did I know that some years later that GOD would place the calling of Preacher and Pastor on my life with a heart and yearning for those looked at as "The Least of These" and Family?

3rd the birth of my children helped me to close the gap of identification. I was adopted by great people into a great family but I longed to see "me". I literally learned about me thru my children. I was so excited to see them in me, when I should have been seeing me in them. When you are discovering who you are, and not having a clear picture of self and you have children, you stand in amazement as if you're the child admiring your parent. So I set out to be the best Dad that I always dreamed of being. My children can go to the Dr.'s office and answer their family history by looking at me, but me as the parent look at them to answer questions about me. Who knew some years down the road this little baby given up for adoption would one day have kids of his own? Who knew some years later my kids would unlock this new level of love that I've never experienced before? Who knew that a once abandoned love would evolve into an Agape love? Little did I know that that some years later I was being molded to become a high school teacher with a gift of listening and the ability to meet the kids "where they are" in life with hopes of giving hope when there seems to be none.

4th forgiving but not forgetting, I've learned that hurt doesn't hurt the one who inflicts the pain but rather the one on the receiving end of the pain. I had to learn to forgive because the truth of the matter is who knows how I would have turned out, who knows where I would have wound up. All I do know is because of the trauma that I experienced, I gained so much more. I was given a family, I was given loving parents, I was put back on the Potter's wheel, heated up, and shaped into what we see today, and for those reasons I must forgive. Holding on to bitterness and hurt was only causing the cracks in this vessel to spread. A crack in in your windshield will get bigger because of sunshine, snow and rain. The constant change from hot to cold and cold to hot. Revelation 3:16 NIV reads "So, because you are lukewarm—neither hot nor cold—I am about to spit you out of my mouth." I had to decide if I was going to forgive or not forgive, did I want to live or die, did I want to stay stuck in the same spot or did I want to move forward in life. I chose life!!! So I forgave, but I will never forget. Well why not Jimmy? Isn't that like straddling the fence, being lukewarm? Why do I say that I will never forget? It is because when you forget where you've come from then your future is injected with too much of self. I choose to remember where I came from to keep me humbled, to keep me dependent upon GOD, to keep my feet in the path that GOD wants me to go. If GOD has not left me yet, If GOD has not failed me yet then I will not put him down just to pick up self.

Remember, I started with telling you that I went to give plasma and found out my blood type, but I didn't tell you something else

111

that I found out. After a little more research I found out that while AB+ blood has both A and B antigens on the red blood cells, neither of the antigens are present in the PLASMA. So this makes AB+ blood type the UNIVERSAL plasma donor, meaning that AB+ plasma can be transfused into patients who have any other A or B or O blood type.

The main role of plasma is to take nutrients, hormones, and proteins to the parts of the body that need it. Cells also put their waste products into the plasma. The plasma then helps remove this waste from the body. Blood plasma also carries all parts of the blood through your circulatory system.

So because of my trauma, what I have to pour into GODS people will help to carry what is needed to strengthen your mind, strengthen your attitude, strengthen your future, and at the same time, it will help you to discard the waste on the inside.

Do You See Me Trying to Breathe? Faith-based journey from the imprisonment of anxiety & panic attacks".

Shekita Jackson

Do you see me trying to breathe? Is this what a heart attack feels like? Will this feeling of suffocation take me out of here? Maybe today, today, is the day that I lose the fight of my life. My heart is pounding out of my chest. Can't they hear it? I can't catch my breath. Do they see me trying to breathe? Can't they see me struggling for air? Sweat covers me as the feeling of being lightheaded overtakes me. I am hoping someone else knows this feeling other than me. I hope I am not the only person that feels this internal constriction in my soul.

Anxiety rushes through the innermost part of me. Panic reaches the depth of my existence. Anxiety is the term given by physicians. A diagnosis of anxiety, wow. A diagnosis of just a feeling to some and an inner turmoil to others. Anxiety is the term that defines what we feel when death seems so near. A medical word that sums up the war that is waging on the inside. A word like none other, with a meaning so ill-defined and vast.

Constant anxiety is an oppressing force in the lives of many people. Most people can't verbalize the struggle that goes on inside of them. Oftentimes, many opt out of expressing the feelings and symptoms they have because they feel that others would call them crazy. Then on top of the current fears and anxieties, more fears are added. In addition, you start to fear sharing your issue because of not wanting to be stigmatized, cast away, or heavily medicated. Anxiety can be a rare occurrence in your life, or even mild. Anxiety can also be excessive and constant.

It was a cold day on the bridge. I was on my way home, but now I am sitting in my car suddenly terrified. Suddenly apprehended by a strange scary feeling. Feeling the wind rocking my car from the numerous cars and tractor-trailers zooming by. I had worked an 8-hour shift in the hospital and was on my way home. I could not figure out why I couldn't make it home. All I knew was that I was having a heart attack. This cannot be happening. I had left the hospital; I left the place that could treat my heart attack. I can't breathe, I am having a heart attack and I need help. I must get help! Someone save me! Let me flag someone down. I get out of the car in rush hour traffic, I must let someone see me. I am waving them down, someone help! In my attempt to calm down while hoping someone else stops to help me, I lay across the back of my car and watch the intense wind-driven waves. I am only separated from the depths of the ocean by a short concrete median on the bridge. I start to scream and yell. How can all these people ride by and see me, and not stop? After what seemed like forever, I hear sirens and I see an ambulance approaching. I am sweating, screaming, and holding my heart.

I am released to go home. They could not find anything wrong with me. Yet, I felt so drained, so weak, so scared. I had my boyfriend get the kids and then come pick me up from the hospital. I couldn't get my head straight to drive. What just happened to me? In a matter of a couple of hours, I had no clue how I went from feeling great to standing outside my car on a long bridge, to back at my job and needing transportation to get home. I was so unaware of the journey I was about to embark on. I had no clue how changed I would become.

Maybe I just needed some rest. I woke up the next day and felt I needed another day of rest and relaxation. A week went by, I still hadn't been out of the home. I still felt off, I had moments where I felt short of breath and very nervous. I went to the ER and again they found nothing clinically wrong and sent me home. Another week, more days of this horrible feeling. Kids are home with me, these days I am scared to be alone. Another night in the ER hoping they would help me, now they sent me home with anti-anxiety medication. I began taking the medication, I took the pills daily for 1-2 weeks and it made me feel like I was in a different reality and with the same high anxiety. I couldn't think clearly, and my family was concerned. Since the high anxiety continued, I stopped taking the medication. Three months went by, and I realized that I had not been to work or outside the home in three months. All the errands and shopping were run by my boyfriend. Three long months in deep fear seem to have come and gone so quickly. Terrified to be alone and scared to be around others, thinking that they would think I have lost my mind and take my children. What has happened to me? I need to get it right.

I'm out! I'm out of the house after three months, we are at my grandmother's apartment. I must be getting over it. I have been feeling like I can breathe and lift my head up for days now. The kids and I are hanging at grandmas. Maybe a change of scenery is what I needed. Since I can remember my grandmother needed to do four things. She worked, went to church, smoked cigarettes, and loved to drink RC cola. My grandmother walked across the street to get some cigarettes and a soda. Not even 10 minutes after she left, I felt an alarm in my soul, I couldn't breathe, and I felt like I was going to pass out. I was too scared to let my girls see me struggling because we were having such a great day. I needed help so I went to my grandma's door to see if she was on her way back home. I didn't see her, and I felt lightheaded, and I was panting. I went to the neighbor's door to ask for help. I knocked and knocked, and no one answered. I went back to my grandma's apartment and bawled up on the couch and cried. I called my boyfriend and he picked us up. I told my grandmother I would see her soon and I went back into my isolation. I had stopped working and stopped going to school. Months later returned to school; I was determined to live.

I am doing the best I can! Months have passed and I didn't know if I was coping or struggling. I felt normal half the time, I felt out of my mind the other half. I went with my baby girl to Walmart to get some items. As soon as I walked in and saw all the hundreds of people in Walmart, I had an instant panic attack and had to hurry to the car. I sat in the car with my daughter in the car seat, and I went through all the motions of my panic attack. When it was over, I went home. I drove home feeling exhausted like I had been in a battle, physically & emotionally.

I am starting to normalize panic attacks and anxiety in my everyday quest to live. I know now when it is coming. I felt the doom coming on fast. I may not be able to fully control my body's reaction to this feeling, and it may be sudden, but I know when it's coming. I am learning how to react. I know that when I am driving to stay in the right lane in case I have a panic attack and need to immediately pull over. I know to take deep breaths and count. I know to talk to myself and tell myself to relax and reassure myself that it won't last long. I know to play my favorite music artist to help my mind stay off my uncontrolled nervousness. I know to be sure to check traffic patterns and drive when it is not rush hour, sitting in traffic for more than a few minutes fueled a panic attack. I know to be around people as much as possible to lessen my panic.

I often wondered if inner turmoil would be with me for the rest of my life. How can anyone live like this forever? I cried out to God often asking for help and safety. The hospitals couldn't help me, they wanted to lock me up because they could not find anything physically wrong with me. No one understood and I couldn't clearly explain every aspect. I was trying to live a productive life as a mom, student, girlfriend, and employee. So many roles and responsibilities, yet daily I struggled to breathe and reconcile my own thoughts. I wanted to be invisible. I screamed silently every day.

Research states that anxiety and panic attacks can start at any time of your life. It can start when you are young or in your adult years. The most interesting and memorable concept is that panic attacks mostly can be a reaction to a traumatic event. The traumatic event could have occurred 1, 5, 10, 20, or 30 years ago. This event has been enclosed inside of you, yet unresolved. Oftentimes one has a traumatic event and later in the years, they feel as though they have moved on. Then when they least expect it, the body joins with the mind and starts expressing or reacting to the traumatic event. The bandage comes off the wound in the form of anxiety & panic attacks. Now your body and mind are not regulated, not secure, and not at peace. The nervous system is on high alert. It's like the body systems start acting out. Your body systems start to let you know that something has violated its peace.

What could that be for me? Could I have suffered an early trauma and now I can no longer suppress it? Maybe it is true. In the research of my life up to that time, I had many eventful moments. We had been removed from my mother's care due to drugs, I and my sister were now living in a household without our baby brother. I didn't know my dad as a kid. I knew what it was like to be hungry. I knew the shame of being in lack among school children. I was a mother at 13 years old. I snuck away and conceived a first-time having sex baby. My life went from child to mother. I had another daughter in my graduating high school senior year. Could any of that cause trauma in my life? Did I not process all that had occurred before age 20? All these years, did I just keep going, keep living?

Which one of these events sounded the alarm in my soul? Why am I now uncontrollably reacting to my past days? The soul can be conflicting. The soul consists of the mind, will, and emotions. All three are connected. I felt like I had lost control of all three. My mind was frightened, and I had a lot of difficulties concentrating. I was an emotional wreck. My emotions changed with the time of day. One moment I wanted companionship or friendship, the next moment I sought isolation. It seemed like my mind, will, and emotions were on one accord to take me out. My soul was tangled. I was fighting for my life.

I am progressing through my college courses, but anxiety is still prevalent. I was determined to learn everything I could and read every book I could find on fear, anxiety, and panic attacks. I frequented the libraries. I always loved to read. I felt that the more I understood what was happening to me, the better my chances of getting back to normal were high. Hopefully, since no one could help me, if I taught myself how to control it, I could heal myself. I was on a mission. I was dedicated to survival. I wanted to thrive. I hoped that one day I would find the right book that would unlock the key to my success and freedom from panic.

The library at my college was so necessary for my weekly routine. Yes, I would have panic attacks there too, I would just quickly go to the bathroom, have my panic attacks, catch my breath, gather myself mentally, then go back to the library to find my healing. My English professor assigned a research paper, she gave us the freedom to select a topic. That was my golden ticket. From the college library to my city's main library, I hunted for research that could teach me and make me whole again. My research paper topic was definitely "causes and cures for anxiety & panic attacks". One particular day in my college library, I saw a classmate of mine from my English class. He was also searching for books that I assumed were for his research assignment. The dark-skinned nice-looking gentleman approached me and stated that he recognized me from class and asked what my research paper topic was. I shared my research topic and he stared at me briefly and he got quiet. He asked me why I wanted to research such a great topic. I quietly shared that I had experienced it, so I wanted to learn more about it. To my surprise, he went on to say that he too experienced anxiety and panic attacks. He now had my full attention.

He led the rest of the conversation. He stated that he was once in Walmart and soon he entered and saw all the people he had a panic attack and immediately went back to his car and left. He told me that he was in the house and had a panic attack and no one was home. He went to the neighbor's house to get help and no one answered, so he went back home and balled up on the couch. He began to tell me of several more accounts. What are the chances that he and I had the exact same panic experiences? He said that he listens to one radio station when driving to help decrease his triggers. He told me to listen to the local gospel station he has been listening to. He then said that he was healed and no longer battles with anxiety because of the promises of God in Psalms 27. He told me to read Psalm 27 daily and as often as I felt anxious. As I listened, I was speechless. In my confusion, I thanked him and left.

Call me a church girl! I grew up in church. He asked me to read Psalms 27 every day when I felt anxious. At that time that meant that I would definitely be reading it every day. I went back and forth in my mind with his prescription of Psalms 27.

119

Psalms 27 was written by David. David birthed these Psalms during a time when he felt deep troubles. A time when David was being haunted by his enemies. He felt that his life was out of control. David went into hiding. He isolated himself. He was hiding by himself, trying to cope with the enemies of his life. He had no peace, and he was anxious because he did not know what tomorrow held for him. David had a pressing enemy; people were looking for him so that they could kill him. He was sad and he was anxious, he was scared. Fear was consuming David. He was wrestling with who he was and all the good moments he had. Now he found himself trying to deal with who he had become. He became a man who was oppressed. He had victories and he had battles. If you live with anxiety and fears, you have days that may be victories and you have days that are battles.

If you or someone you know wrestles with anxiety, remind them that anxiety is not a part of God's design for their life. It is not a part of what God wants for you. It is not how God wants you to live. Anxiety is a thief and a robber. It creates a stronghold on your life that is designed to choke every ounce of peace from you. Robbing you of your peace and confidence in who you are. Most times we can't even define a clear reason to be anxious. We often have no idea of the thing that first shook us on the inside. Professionals can help steer us toward tracking the root because oftentimes we can't trace what initiated that internal struggle. This is because when life happens to us, we suppress it, and we keep on living.

Every day is an opportunity for a fresh wind and healing of our soul (mind, will, emotions). God grants us that opportunity every day we wake up. He grants us the love, mercy, and grace that we need to heal. Psalms 27, provides us the opportunity for peace in our emotions. ***Vs 1 "With him on my side, I am fearless, afraid of no one and nothing".***
It is God who gives us the strength to live free from anxiety. Doctors can medicate you, but God can deliver you. God already

knows the plans that he has for you, yet they can't become fully tangible while you are living scared, while you are captive to anxieties. It is God that makes the captives free. You can have control of negative thoughts. You can have control over nervous behaviors.

Anxiety will leave a stronghold in your entire household if you don't get free. Anxiety can grip your entire generation if you don't become free. God is the only one who can strengthen you past your ability to cope and manage your fears and manage your wondering thoughts. Anxiety will have you anticipating the worst. Anxiety will make you afraid to be alone with yourself or uncomfortable around other people. Anxiety is an enemy that fights relentlessly for your soul, it keeps you struggling with yourself. You struggle to stop thinking about society & circumstances that are out of your control. You become less lovable because you feel too powerless to love.

Anxiety wants to deliberately damage that work that God has started in you. Anxiety is an aggressive invader that seeks to steal and take over your life. Bit by bit, circumstances eat away at our peace. If not exposed and dealt with properly, they become hidden and suppress emotions and feelings. Bit by bit the enemy attacks, small trauma after small trauma, relationship after relationship, health issue after health issue. All these things make a well inside of you. One day you become unsettled with yourself. It is the power of God that settles us.

In the text, David felt like an army was against him. Another biblical translation states that he felt besieged meaning David felt surrounded by forces that were aiming to capture him and force him to surrender to them. When David surrendered his anxieties to God, David says *"IM CALM AS A BABY"*. David began to be collected and cool as he allowed himself to be reassured of the promises of God. Whatever state you find yourself in, be collected & be cool. Know that your redeemer lives. Anxiety comes to distract you. Remember, you can't fulfill God's purpose for your life if you are fearful. David talked to God, he said ***"I am asking God for one thing"***. If you can only ask God for one thing, what would it be?

Angels Unaware

God is the only quiet secure place in a noisy world. I have been feeling better the last few days. I am starting to function better. I am working my normal shifts. As the days go by, I am driving more. The best thing of all is that I have found joy at home, and I have been responding well to my kids and friends this past week. Could it be that by reading Psalms 27 daily, I would feel like I am coming out of deep water?

A short time has passed, but I can't wait to get to English class to share with the guy that he has helped me. I am still baffled about how close our actual experiences are. I arrived in class a little early so I could chat with him before class started. He didn't arrive early so I went to my seat. Class started and he still wasn't there. Class ended and he never arrived. This saddened me because I really wanted to share my progress with him. I couldn't remember his name. When class was over, I went to the teacher to ask her for the gentleman's first name. I asked her and she stated that she didn't recall that student. I pointed to where he usually sits, and she told me that no one had sat in that seat in the entire semester. I provided more descriptions of his features and she persistently told me that no one with those features was in the class and that seat had been empty. She claimed to know her students. How can this be? I went to the library to see if he was there doing research, no success. Okay, maybe the teacher was confused. The next week the same thing happened, and that seat remained empty for the duration of the semester.

Hebrews 13:2 KJV says, "Be not forgetful to entertain strangers: for thereby some have entertained angles unawares"

I was even more confused. I have heard of "entertaining angels unaware". I have heard people tell of their own accounts of what could only be explained as an angel sent from God. As a child, we were always told that we have guardian angels that are assigned to watch over us. I saw a classmate and then later met him in the library. I had met a gentleman that looks like an everyday guy. He shared a disorder and chronic issue that I was currently dealing with. He told of very similar accounts of fear and panic. He then gave me instructions on how to take back control of my life. He re-introduced me to Jesus, the savior of my soul. He gave me a roadmap to freedom from the internal prison I was held in. The tools he gave me were really working. I was starting to have small daily victories, and I just wanted to share that victory with him.

What are the chances that I could have met an angel? Even more interesting, why would I receive one? I am a nobody. I am a young single mother who solely supports my children on my slightly above minimum wage job. We survive paycheck to paycheck, earning enough for very basic needs. Why would I deserve to be sent an angel from God? I have not prayed regularly, haven't tithed regularly, nor have I attended church service regularly. Yet, I have been given a strange encounter that is changing my life. I felt like hope had sprung up from a dry well.

The Road to Freedom
"There is no greater agony than bearing an untold story inside you."
— Maya Angelou

Stories go untold so often due to the owner of the story fearing how others would respond. Not wanting to face the opinions of others. For this reason, stories of freedom from life oppressions go untold. Living with chronic anxiety, fears, and frequent panic attacks can for some be a story untold. Who wants to freely share their inner terrors and secret uncertainties? Would those close to you mock you or try to disregard how you feel, or would strangers cast their opinions? The decision to tell someone about the deep and misunderstood feelings that are inside of you is the most freeing thing you can do. That's the start of your healing. Expressing the good and bad emotions that rage inside of you releases the hold that oppressive anxiety has on you. Share your untold story. You can live a life free from the restraints of anxiety disorders. Some may feel anxious from time to time their entire life. Prayer, meditation, and therapy can be of great assistance to learning your triggers. I have learned that if I am not well-rested that I will begin to feel anxious. I have learned that the word of God soothes my soul. I also know that bridges are not my favorite place, and it may take some deep breathing and music to keep me comfortable. I no longer avoid anxiety conversations. I still depend on Psalms 27 in any translation. I have also added to my arsenal Psalms 91. I feel free to live and free to breathe. I am no longer hiding in my own prison. I am also not ashamed of sharing my story. This story has strengthened me, and it is my hope that this book has strengthened you.

I Had to Adjust My Crown Time & Time Again

———————————

By Anita Jeter-Peterkin

As I sit here listening to light jazz, taking in the aroma of lilac scented candles, the energy in the room becomes prolific. Melodic melodies soothe my soul as I reach for the tilted crown slanted to the right side of my head. Being aware of its position, I straighten it with ease. Gently protecting the vortex of its being. Amazed at the times this invisible crown has been adjusted because of insinuating circumstances, truly blows my mind.

Ever since I was a child, I had dreams to brighten the world with thoughts that ran through my vivid imagination. I imagined owning a business, creating artwork and sharing my life stories through poetic words flowing from mind, to pen to paper. I found my passion and purpose without even knowing it. The mere things I dreamed about are now the amazing things I do through my businesses and community initiatives, and that is to serve and inspire others through creative arts.

My crown is my vortex. It is the place where my mind connects to energy and vibrations which allows me to create and cultivate through different forms of art. By the Grace of GOD, the energy is what supplies my strength and empowers me to overcome obstacles, jump hurdles and climb mountains. Not only am I granted permission to dream, but I have also been able to capture my dreams and bring them to life.

My vision, passion and purpose are all wrapped up into one dream, which is to inspire and bring hope to those who are on the verge of giving up and throwing in the towel. My crown has tilted multiple times in life and as I straighten it to regroup and reignite, I'm reminded of how my journey all began. I'm reminded of how I had to push through the fire.

No one ever said it would be easy, but I knew deep down inside, if I wanted it bad enough it was doable. Therefore, I learned to push through the fire, straighten my crown and adjust my attitude so I would be able to walk in my purpose and speak to my truth. But hold on! Remember, I said no one ever said it would be easy. And this is how my story goes.

Are Princesses Really Crowned?

I may not have known it then, but as a little girl my vortex began to develop as my imagination soared high as the deep blue skies. A purposeful ball of energy surrounded my thoughts capturing all the small and sometimes humungous dreams buried within. I remember riding in the back of the brown paneled station wagon, gazing out the windows in deep thoughts about what I would like to be when I grew up. Those moments were priceless.

There were at least three major things I dreamed of doing when I was a child. I wanted to teach, own my own business and encourage others to believe they could do anything they wanted through creative forms of art. My desire to teach came from helping my siblings with their studies. My mom did not have to ask twice about helping them, I was eager for the opportunity to teach them what I knew and to watch them learn. I believe teaching has always been a part of who I am. Although, I never became a schoolteacher, I had the honor to substitute for two years at an elementary and high school.

When it came to encouraging others to dream and to believe in themselves, I was the one to turn to. I remember creating plays, choreographing dance and then having my siblings and cousins audition for the roles or dance spots. They all believed that someday we would perform on Soul Train or The American Band Stand. They practiced long and hard to make the cuts and was excited to be a part of the production when their names were called. My mother had instilled in me that I could be anything I wanted, and I intended to spread the exact same thing to anyone who would listen.

I still remember the days I dreamed of owning my own business as a little girl. Watching the old black and white movies as I sat on the sofa with my mom is still clear in my mind. I remember asking her about the men who were in the movies always carrying brief cases and seemed to visit the banks more often than any other characters in the movie. My mom would explain to me who the men where, what they did and the significance of their roles as actors as well as in real life situations.

My first thoughts where, I wanted to be just like them. I wanted to work for myself, provide for my family and live a happy life. What an imagination for a little girl, or should I say Princess? I believe, that was when my vortex began to form within the core of my crown. This was when the energy of the Universe heard my thoughts and saw beyond my vision. This is when my tiara was exchanged for the crown I would wear so proudly. My crown would now harbor the vortex of energy molding my faith, hope, and determination to be all I would dream to become.

As a child life was great. I was a military brat and had the opportunity to travel out of the country and to a few states in the US. Meeting new people and having the ability to experience other cultures and communities was great for me as a child. It's part of what has formed me into the woman I am today. Feeling like the little Princess without a worry or care in the world, would soon come to a pause.

Life, as I saw it, had begun to change and everything seemed to be falling apart. It seems just like yesterday that I saw my dad walk out of our door for the last time. It was unimaginable as a child that a parent would walk away to never return to his or her family. This was the first time I felt that tiara turned crown tilt slowly down my head. Years later as a teen the vortex would have to embellish my crown and provide everything needed to face life's curveballs and more.

My energy was low, but the vortex began to build and a create space within my crown to face and conquer the challenges of life to come. For the next few years, the trajectory of my path would change and give me the roller coaster ride of my life. Soon several major events would impact my life forever and cause my crown to tilt and even at times fall from my head. These events could have caused me to give up and throw in the towel of life. However, GOD empowered me to straighten that crown time and time again, so I could live the life I desired to live.

Crown Down Impact #1 Dropping Out of School

As I reminisce of how my adolescent life began, I'm amazed at how GOD covered and protected me through it all. After my dad and mom separated, I was able to see the strengths and truth of my mom. She had to take on the role of many, including the provider and the protector. I watched her leave for work every morning heading to a long day of labor. At first, I must admit, I was a little embarrassed to see her going in for work to drive a trash truck. I thought my mom to be worthy of something better in life. Like a secretary or a teacher. The nerve of me! Yet, I could only imagine one day retiring my mom from her job so she could live happier, but the truth is my mom loved what she did and the people on her route loved her. She was happy and content with her career and life.

Seeing my mom straighten her crown every single day, inspired me to follow in her footsteps when life got tough. One of the things my mom would always say and stuck with me until today is "you can be anything you want to be." She was my biggest supporter in everything I did and always encouraged me to keep on keeping on. Mom was there through the thick and thin. She never gave up on me no matter what the circumstances were. Without her, I would have been lost.

As my mom took on the major roles in our home, I began to start feeling myself. I started hanging out, skipping school and doing the opposite of what I had been raised to do. At one point my mom sent me to stay with my dad in Fayetteville North Carolina, but that only lasted a couple of months. I began to feel sick a lot. Nausea and vomiting every morning. Low and behold, when I went to get a physical for cheerleading tryouts, I found out I was pregnant. I was only fifteen years old.

My dad was not happy at all and sent me back home to my mom. I did not know how I would face telling my mom the news. I thought of how she would respond and believe me they were not positive at all, but when I returned home to Virginia, my mom showed me nothing but love and support. She was not disappointed in me, but she did have a long talk with me about my new responsibilities. Although, my mom explained to me how important it was to stay in school and earn my diploma, I thought I knew what was best for me. After hearing some students talking about me and my pregnancy, I decided I did not want to go to school anymore. I thought I was smart enough to get a job and earn a living to take care of my newborn child, along with my boyfriend. It did not take long for me to see how smart I truly was not. I received interviews over the phone, but once I showed up, it was a different story. No one wanted to hire a drop out, especially a young Black woman with a newborn baby without an education.

Years later, one of our community mentors discussed the possibility of me returning to school. I was against going back to my high school because I was embarrassed and did not want to face my peers. When my mentor suggested earning my GED, I really did not want to do that either. I thought I was too smart to be connected to a so-called GED. I was an honor roll-student, but I knew that would be the only way I would be able to further my education without going back to my high school. After months of contemplating, I eventually took the suggestion of my mentor and registered for the GED program. I studied and passed the course for my General Education Diploma and felt accomplished.

Crown Adjusted #1-Adjust that Attitude

Dropping out of school haunted me for years. I was a good student and really loved school. Unfortunately, I let my pride get in the way and it caused me to take a longer and harsher road to earning a higher education. I truly, felt a GED was beneath me and I could do without it. That thought was the furthest from the truth. Earning my GED would prove to be one of the best choices I made in my life. After earning my GED, I became determined to pursue a higher education. I studied at a local community college and earned my Associates Degree in Business management. I knew I had to push forward after being denied several office positions I had applied for. I did not know if I was being rejected because of my lack of experience, education, and race or because I was a young mother from the projects. I refused to allow any of those circumstances stop me from pursuing the life I wanted to live.

Years later I enrolled in UMUC for the bachelor's program. It took longer than normal to earn my B.A. because I was a part-time student. Earning my B.A allowed me to grow in the field of sales and management. I worked for great organizations but always wanted to own a business and invest in myself as I did for other businesses. Then one day, I was offered an entrepreneurship opportunity and the rest is history with owning my own business. I started multiple MLM businesses and enjoyed serving others as well as assisting them to start their own businesses or side hustles.

After the tilting of my crown, I was able to adjust it more. My vortex kept building the foundation and walls in a special space to allow me to flourish during troubled times. Pushing through the fire was a challenge, yet it was doable because I became empowered to refocus and adjust when needed. Having the ability to push, to keep on keeping on and to adjust that tilted crown allowed me to capture many of my dreams. I am now a published author of five books, inspirational speaker, artist and own my online art gallery. I also utilized those flames to service others through my Wrapped-N-Pink Breast Cancer Awareness Organization and my I AM... movement and initiative. I am grateful for these humble beginnings and will never forget how I arrived at such a special place in my life. I give GOD all the praise, because when I think back to being a teen mom, it amazes me as to far I have truly come.

Crown Down Impact #2-Teen Mom

After moving back to Virginia and informing my mom and boyfriend about my pregnancy, I had to make big decisions. My life went from being a fifteen-year-old teenager to becoming a sixteen-year-old woman real fast. There was no doubt in my mind as to whether I would go on with my pregnancy, but I knew doing so would change my life forever. There would be no more hanging out at the skating rink, running to the mall with friends or lying around doing nothing all day. Lessons of life was about to kick in strong. I lived with my mom, but I always felt like I had to do the grown-up thing and get my own place and take care of my own responsibilities.

I also wanted to try college and earn my degree, but that would prove much more of a challenge than I had imagined. I had to find a babysitter, apply for student loans, get a ride to campus and so much more that it became overwhelming. I decided to put those dreams on hold until I could tie up the loose ends. I wanted to do something with my life, but it was hard being a young mother. For the next three years after having my first child, I had two more children. By the time I had turned eighteen, I was a young mother of three without an education or a fulltime job. I had become a young uneducated welfare recipient living in the projects.

According to society, I was doomed because I had made some real bad choices, and I probably would have been, if I had listened to its voices. I was determined to only use the welfare system as a stepping-stone to my success. Yet, at times it was hard to break away from free food stamps, low-income housing, free health and childcare. Every time I would take one step forward the system would pull me back, attempting to hold me hostage to a hostile environment. The projects were my destination for equal housing, because luxurious homes and beautiful estates were only for my browsing. At times it looked like there would be no way out.

Although, I do not knock the system, I must say it had the ability to persuade me to fear moving toward success because the sacrifices were unbearable at times. To earn a few dollars more than allowed in the system could have made the difference of having food and shelter for my family and moving back in with my mom. I did my best to take care of my children. Sometimes I worked two to three jobs at a time to make ends meet. I again realized how much better life would be with a college degree or trade. I knew the sacrifice would be significant, but the reward would be greater. My crown was slipping. My vortex was rising. It was time to adjust to the changes of life.

Crown Adjusted #2 Being Responsible

My mother made sure she did not interfere with me becoming a responsible parent. She would assist with my babies when needed, but she never became a crutch that would allow me to relinquish my duties of raising my children. Momma Ruth was my greatest supporter, advisor and confidant during a time when life was filled with lots of uncertainty. My crown was once again tilted from the decisions I had made, but my Vortex continued to build confidence, hope and determination within the realm of this special space. I was ready to face those challenges head on and move to bigger and better things in life. I knew it would not be easy, but I felt it would be doable. Being focused with a purpose in mind would lead me to a road of success.

It was time to adjust my crown and begin to create a life I truly wanted to live. As a parent, I made education an essential part of my children's life and participated in every event they were a part of. From Head Start to College, I was determined to be as involved with their educational journey as possible.

As my children soared through elementary school, I thought it was time to be a good example in their life. It was time for me to get an education of my own. I went from being a high school drop out to earning my first degree at about twenty-two years old. At this point in my life, I had my own apartment, I was a college graduate and had a fulltime job. My children were well taken care of and they were thriving in school and had all the basics of life. This year was one of the most productive and happy years I had experienced in my life, but that was soon to change.

That year I was turning twenty-three my crown would tilt again. It tilted so far to the side of my head that it almost fell. It almost caused me to give up because what was about to happen to me as a twenty-two-year-old woman was very uncommon in the USA. My life about to change once again as I pushed through the fire.

Crown Down Impact #3-One year to live

Although, things were coming along in my life, there was another curveball waiting to hit me like a boulder. One day my friend saw a little bump on my lefts side between my arm and breast area. She suggested I get it checked out, but I truly felt like it was nothing. I was young and in fit mint condition. I felt, I had nothing to worry about. Soon after, my mom saw the bump and told me to get myself to the doctor and get it checked out. I finally set an appointment and got myself in. As waited in the dark dainty room, I could only imagine what would have been discovered. I was examined by three doctors and each one asked the same questions. How many children do you have? How old are you? Does your family have breast cancer history?

The questioning was making me worry. My grandmother was a survivor of breast cancer, but I did not know much about it, because it was never really talked about. After answering their questions, one doctor scheduled me for a return visit to perform a biopsy. I asked him what a biopsy was, and he explained he'd have to stick a needle in my breast to see what was really going on inside of me.

I thought to myself, he must be out of his cotton-picking mind. Although, the appointment was scheduled, I knew I would not return for the procedure. I waited a year to return to the doctor's office. That little itty-bitty bump had turned into a full-size lump. My doctor scheduled an emergency surgery for the next week. I would be turning twenty-three. Before surgery, my doctors had me sign paperwork, explaining it was a strong possibility that I may have breast cancer and possibly lose my left breast. I signed the paperwork and thought the chances of losing my breast was not going to happen. But my thoughts would prove to be wrong. My crown tilted and tilted, while my vortex strengthened.

As my doctors entered the room, I could sense the report would not be favorable. Although, my mom had told me I was praising GOD and thanking HIM for another chance at life as they rolled me out of the operation room, I was afraid of what they were about to reveal to me. Just as I imagined, my doctor told me I was diagnosed with breast cancer, and they had to remove my left breast. I was scared, afraid and I was uncertain about what my life would be like after my diagnosis. I was only twenty-three. But my doctors were not finished with reviewing my report. As he looked down in sadness, my doctor also told me I had a poor prognosis and would probably not survive a year.

My heart dropped! My life flashed in front of me so rapid that I couldn't make out a single thing. I began to cry and yell out GOD! Please LORD! No! The first thing that came to mind was who would take care of my children and how they would face life without a mom. I was devastated, but my mom was right there by my side and comforted me throughout the day. I thought to myself, I have to have faith and believe GOD for a miracle. My crown was falling, but my vortex kept rising to catch my fall.

Crown Adjusted #3 From Fear to Faith, Trust & Hope

Once again, life had thrown another curveball my way. The week after my surgery was supposed to be one of the best days of my life. I had earned my Associates Degree and would walk across the stage to receive a diploma for the first time in my life. This was important to my family and me. The time was to be full of celebrations, instead I was dealing with facing a death sentence from the Big C...Cancer. I had to figure out a way to adjust my crown and move beyond the uncertainty. The first thing I had to do was pray and put it all in GOD's hands. I had to dig deep down and depend on GOD for a cure. I had to have Faith and Trust that everything would go according to GOD's plans. I had to move from fear and have faith in GOD.

The first year was like being on a roller coaster ride. I had to go through a year of chemotherapy, months of radiation, losing my hair, my breast and waking up some days wondering if it would be my last day of life. But GOD covered and saved me. HE gave me another chance at life. He put me on a path to share my testimony and bring hope to others.

I realized GOD had missioned me to do work through creative forms of art, because art had not only become my passion it had become a cause. I started writing poetry, speaking at events about breast cancer awareness and dabbling in drawings and paintings. Not realizing what I was being led to do, I decided to start an organization to inspire other breast cancer survivors. That is when my Wrapped-N-Pink Breast Cancer Awareness Organization was birthed.

Through my organization I was able to host workshops, perform one-woman monologues, write books about my journey, host breast cancer awareness walks, fund raisers and speak about my journey of surviving breast cancer by the Grace of GOD to different organizations. I leaned in to push through the fire. I adjusted my crown as my vortex strengthened.

For years I persevered through the storms of life. I pushed through the fire, time and time again. And life kept on happening with the good and the bad, the wins and the losses which would show up once again.

Crown Down Impact #4-Curve Balls

Pushing through the fire may create many variables that will not only challenge your faith but also challenge your willingness to keep on keeping on. Life's curveballs will come and go. It's not about when they will come, but more so about how you will react or respond to them when they arrive.

I've had many curveballs come my way, but none of them hit me as hard as losing my mom. My mother was my rock, my biggest supporter, my confidant and my living angel. When mom departed this earth, I felt she took a part of me. I was sad that she would not see me earn my master's degree and begin the Doctoral Program to earn my Doctorate Degree. After all, she was the force behind me pursuing a higher education.

My mom had truly molded me to become the woman I am today. Yet, she would not get to witness it. I thank GOD that HE allowed my fathers to remain in my life and they were able to pick up where she left off. Life continues to happen, and fires continues to exist in my life. Fires such as losing our baby, losing a six-figure job, losing my marriage and permanent disabilities from injuries caused by accidents. It's evident that my crown will tilt ever now an again, but with faith, determination, perseverance and hope my vortex has created, I'm destined to achieve great things.

Crown Adjusted #4 5 Stages to Push Through the Fire

My stories of pushing through the fire are my testimonies of how GOD covered, protected and guided me through trials and tribulations. Although, my crown tilted, it never fell. My crown is strengthened by my vortex, a special happening within my mind, body and soul to allow me to persevere and move beyond my circumstances.

I went through five stages to push through each fire event:
> (1) I had to first and foremost call on the LORD to equip me to face, fight and not fear each fire I was experiencing.

(2) I had to hold myself accountable for the choices I made, which may have created the fires.

(3) I grieved, I cried, I got angry, I allowed myself to feel the emotions and to experience the pain of each fire.

(4) But I did not stay there. I refocused my energy to forgive myself and others so I could create the life I wanted to live. I adjusted my crown when needed.

(5) By the Grace of GOD, I was determined to turn those tragedies into triumphs by sharing what I went through and how I got through it with others. I leaned into my Vortex, the space which strengthened my crown to protect my mind, body and soul.

There will always be fires in life. The question is not when will it come? The question is how will you push through it? Will you allow the energy of your Vortex to equip your crown to strengthen you and to guide you? Will you trust GOD and put it all in HIS hands?

From the Fields to the Stage

_____

Skip Bailey

This was written to tell the truth, the whole truth and nothing but the truth. It's been said that the truth will set you free; well I hope that by telling my story and my truth, I will help you to understand that your truth may just be what someone else needs to hear.

In this excerpt of From The Fields to the Stage, I will be uncovering some deep down buried issues and situations I've experienced in my life, I've allowed to keep me from moving forward and achieving my goals and dreams in the past.

I was born in Capeville, Virginia July 13, 1958 in my great grandmother's house, which had no running water or inside bathroom. Capeville, Virginia is thirty-seven miles from Virginia Beach, and only three minutes just before the Chesapeake Bay tunnel toll entrance. So, whenever you go to Virginia Beach via. Route #13 South, you will pass by my hometown, but don't blink, you'll miss it.

While living in Virginia as a little boy, I often remember times when me and my little brother and sister would have to go to the potato fields with my grandmother. We went to the potato fields with my grandmother because often times that's how she earned money; it was her job. She would take me, my brother and sister with her, because there was no one to watch us when she had to go to work. I learned how to pick potatoes and other vegetables such as corn, lima beans, tomatoes, cabbage, strawberries and other vegetables at the age of seven to earn money to live on.

The reason me and my siblings were with our grandmother was the fact that our parents had moved to New Jersey to find employment, so my grandmother agreed to keep us in Virginia until my parents were able to send for us. Most of the time, me my siblings and our cousins would pile in the back of my uncle's pickup truck to catch a ride to the fields. I guess we had fun and enjoyed riding in the back of the pickup truck back then, besides we really didn't have a choice that was our way of life. I learned how to pull potatoes up from the dirt after the plow had lifted them up from under the surface of the dirt. The excess dirt had to be knocked off the potatoes which were then placed into a wooden basket. As I grew a year older and a little stronger, I was able to empty the potatoes from the basket into a burlap sack bag, which was tied and placed on a wagon being pulled by a tractor.

While living in Virginia, I would often wake up cold and wet. The reason for the coldness was the fact that we did not have heat in every room of our house. As a matter of fact, we only had direct heat in the living room of our house. The houses built back then did not have central heating or heating supply in different rooms of the houses, so we would nearly always sleep with our bedroom doors open.

The other reason that I would wake up cold and wet was because of my bedwetting issue. There were many nights that I would try to stay awake as long as I could so that I would not wake up in a cold wet spot in my bed. There were times as a young boy I would tie a shoestring around my penis hoping it would stop my bed wetting issue.

My grandmother and my parents did not know what the cause of my bedwetting issue was, all they knew was that I did not get up in the middle of the night to go to the bathroom. I was constantly fussed at because they had to wash my bed sheets a few times a week, and I'm not talking about going to the laundromat or having the luxury of having a washer and dryer in our house, because we did not have access to neither of them.

Speaking of bathrooms, our house did not have a toilet, we had a waste bucket that we used to relieve ourselves which had to be taken outside to the outhouse to empty, which we'll discuss later. I experienced my bedwetting issue for many years and did not know the reason for it. As an adult, I discussed it with a family member and was told that it might have been a hereditary issue for some of the older males in our family. I am thankful that those issues have moved on many years ago, but I have also learned that my past bedwetting issue as a child into early teen years may have contributed to lack of confidence in the past. I was in denial for so long and buried my hurt and insecurities so well, no one ever knew that I was being held hostage by my past issue. I looked good on the outside, but on the inside I was damaged. It's one thing being beat up by someone else but beating yourself up mentally leaves unnoticeable and untraceable scars rarely noticed by others.

There is a saying that goes, 'I'm not telling you what I've heard, I'm telling you what I know'. I know that if you begin to acknowledge and face the present and past issues that you may have, you will be able to start to release some of the inner issues which may have been holding you hostage also. For myself, I know that I buried my issues and covered them up with so many nice-looking things that most of the time, I forgot that my past bedwetting issue was still buried deep-down in me. I covered and buried my past issues when dating a lot of girls, and later on, dating a lot of women. Dating was part of my bandage.

There was the time where my thoughts led me to a seed planted in me which gave me the desire to be on stage. It began at our little town dance hall. The place was called The Hall, which was located just down the road from our house; note that I did say, just down the road. The Hall was where everyone went on Friday, Saturday, and Sunday afternoons.

If you've ever heard of a juke joint, the hall was a modern-day juke joint. Prior to becoming the town dance hall, my mother told me that The Hall was once a school, and years later became a place where area residents would go to receive minor medical care. That was before my time, so I only know it as The Hall. When my mother and father would come back to Virginia on weekends to see me and my siblings, they would always take us there, the Hall was really the only place to go on weekends. There were adults and children down at The Hall, and there was always the smell of cigarettes, cheap beer and whiskey in the air. Though there was no air conditioning to keep it cool in the hot summer days, windows were open and maybe a fan in the window for ventilation, it did not stop the activities happening at The Hall.

During the winter months my parents would take us there where there was no gas or electric heat supply. The only heat source was a large black cast iron stove which was constantly filled with coal or wood to supply the heat. The adults would be drinking whiskey, wine and beer, and some of the nonalcoholic drinkers and the children would be drinking soda pop. The truth is, every now and then, some of the children would have a sip of beer, which was given to them by a relative. Everyone would be dancing and having good time on the dance floor, adults and children. Even though it was hot in there, especially in the summertime, we were having the time of our lives.

At The Hall, the jukebox would be playing the latest songs and when my favorite songs would come on by my favorite artist, James Brown, I was ready to hit the floor. I would dance until I got tired or until the jukebox played a slow record. While on the dance floor dancing, the adults would gather around to watch some of us children do our thing, so I made sure that I was getting most of the attention. I would be spinning, sliding, the split, grinding and any other dance moves that I could come up with. Yes, I was grinding on the dance floor! Between the ages of six and nine years old I was doing adult dance moves, and I had everyone's attention. I guess that's where Black Silk got his start. We'll talk about him later.

When we moved to New Jersey, it took me a while to adjust to city living because I knew nothing about the city at all. I had to adjust to living on a street verses living on a road where there were no traffic lights and very few stop signs. Some of my first trips to New Jersey, after crossing the Delaware Memorial Bridge seeing the lights, I would ask if all the lights were New York City?

We lived in the East Trenton section, and I became friends with Butch and Lee Flowers. After I made a few friends, I joined the local Police Athletic League (PAL) little league. I played for the Red Sox baseball team as a pitcher and the first baseman. I had a real talent for baseball, and it was the only sport I played in Virginia as a little boy. My father and my uncles played baseball while growing up in Virginia and they also played on a few minor league baseball teams in New Jersey.

Growing up I was around baseball all the time, so playing the sport came naturally. Living in Virginia, my cousins and I played baseball when we weren't in school or helping in the fields. We played in the front yard, the backyard, in the road and even in the field when the crops had been plowed down. During a community block party, I had the opportunity to hear live music being played by a local band, and after witnessing the band's performance, I was hooked! My friends, Butch and Lee were from a musical family. Butch played lead guitar and Lee played the drums. I wanted to learn how to play the guitar and my nurturing parents knew too, so for Christmas I got a guitar. I was determined to learn how to play the guitar. We had an idea to start a band but there were a few issues; I had not learned how to play the guitar well and we had two guitar players, no bass guitarist. Butch already knew how to play the lead guitar, I had to learn how to play the bass guitar. Another issue was that I did not have a bass guitar, so I had to turn my lead guitar into a bass guitar. Bass guitar strings are thicker than regular guitar strings, so my father had to drill bigger holes in the area where the strings were placed in the guitar so that the larger bass guitar strings would fit. We went to a store called Two Guys and purchased a set of cheap six-dollar bass guitar strings, and that's how my bass guitar career began. Butch and Lee first taught me how to play the bass guitar, and I later had lessons from their cousin James, who was a good bass guitarist who lived around the corner from us. About a year later after rehearsing in their parents' basement and at times rehearsing in my parents' basement, I had my first opportunity to perform on stage in the 7th grade at a school event.

After about a year or so, Lee began to focus more on baseball. He played drums but Lee was a great baseball pitcher. He taught me a lot about being a good baseball pitcher. I played baseball in the seventh and eighth grade in junior high school, where only ninth graders were allowed to be the starting pitcher on the team. I was good enough to be the first seventh grader to start at pitcher at Junior High School #1 in Trenton, New Jersey. During this time, I started to hang with some of the older guys in the area, and was introduced to wine, marijuana and cigarettes. I had never heard of marijuana until I moved to New Jersey because as I mentioned earlier, I had only been exposed to cigarettes, beer and whiskey. There were many weekend house parties back then, and there were a few times that I drank wine and beer at the parties and had to walk home under the influence of alcohol. I knew that my parents were disappointed with me during those times, but I was still fairly new to city life and was being influenced by older boys that I should not have been hanging with.

Not too long after being introduced to different elements, people, and negativity, I stopped playing baseball because I was starting to get a lot of attention from the girls. I had gone from being a little country boy from the south to moving to the city becoming one of the popular kids in the school, but I was totally out of my element. Where I come from, there were not a lot of people and the girls were only African American. We moved to the city where there were Blacks, Hispanics and other ethnic groups too. I can remember times when our family would be preparing to go to Virginia for a weekend visit, and my mother had to force me to go because I did not want to leave my current environment in the city. At the time, I felt that there was nothing for me to go back to Virginia for, not even to visit relatives. I was hooked on city life and the city girls!

During my last year in junior high school, we moved to West Trenton, and that's where it really began to heat up. Living in East Trenton, I thought I had seen my share of pretty girls but moving to West Trenton had taken me to a whole different level. Moving just to the other side of town as a musician was like opening the door to a candy store. I already had admirers from East and North Trenton, but moving to West Trenton caused my ego shoot up five levels higher. By the time I started high school, I was smoking marijuana more often along with going to weekend house parties more than before. Some of the musicians in the area found out that I was a bass guitar player and asked me if I wanted to join their band. One of the first guys who approached me was Reggie Dash, who played drums in the West Trenton area. Reggie was the nephew of Sara Dash, who was a member of the singing group LaBelle. We'd rehearse in Reggie's mother's basement a few times a week, and during every rehearsal there were always a few people standing outside on the sidewalk listening to us practice, mostly girls.

At one point I decided I wanted to change my appearance to a popular style, and I asked my mother to perm my hair. She was a hair stylist. I wanted to look like some of the guys in the Super Fly movie. I was really beginning to go all the way out. There was a store downtown where a lot of guys shopped, so I asked my mother to buy me a blue sparkled three-piece suit. I remember the day that I wore my blue sparkled three-piece suit to school and my friend Chucky wore his blue suit. We were like celebrities! Being musicians and wearing those suits to school, we took school popularity to another level!

There was one incident when the four of us were parked across the street from the high school on a side street smoking marijuana. There was so much smoke in the car, it looked like a scene from a Cheech and Chong movie. It was cold outside, and our body heat along with the smoke made the windows really hard to see out of. I looked in the rearview mirror and saw a police vehicle coming down the street, so we immediately told Chucky not to panic and don't roll down window. Well, we might as well have told him to make sure he rolled the window down! As soon as the police car got next to us, he panicked and rolled the window down! Smoke was everywhere just like in a Cheech and Chong movie, but luckily the police officer didn't see the smoke. We picked on him and teased him for months about almost getting us arrested.

As a teenager, I played in a lot of bars and a few clubs in New Jersey. We played in a lot of bars in Trenton. One of the bars we played in frequently was The Cove, located downtown Trenton. To get inside of the bar we had to go downstairs to the main entrance, I think there was only one in and one way out. Even though we played in a lot of bars, we did not drink alcohol while we were performing. Another bar we performed in was the Cadillac Club in Philadelphia, PA. We performed there a few times because our manager knew the owner. One night, a lady asked me if I wanted to come home with her, because she said that her husband was affiliated with MFSB, Mother/Father Sister/Brother, musicians based at Philadelphia's Sigma Sound Studio. Not too long after performing in Philadelphia, we had the opportunity to perform at the Baby Grand Lounge in New York.

One summer our band was preparing to travel to Virginia to perform at my family reunion during the day and were to perform later in the evening at a small place that my father and cousin was running. The band that I was performing with at the time was a backup band for a singing group called the Revells. We scheduled extra rehearsals preparing to be very sharp to perform in front of our new audience. We made all the preparations to make our very first performance in Virginia perfect. We made sure that all the equipment was working properly, we had our uniforms dry cleaned and placed in carrying bags. We rented a van to transport the equipment along with a few of the band members. Everything seemed to be set in place, but there was one thing we overlooked; how do we get to Virginia, and who was going to drive the equipment van. None of the members had ever been to Virginia before and I was the only one who knew how to get there. I said that I would drive the van. The members in the singing group were adults and all the musicians were all teenagers, me being the youngest at seventeen. We all agreed that I would drive. The fact that I did not have a driver's license and did not look like an adult didn't stop the plan we had come up with.

We went downtown to the store where I purchased my blue sparkled three-piece suit. We bought an apple-jack hat and a pair of sunglasses I could wear to help disguise my youthful look. My apple-jack hat was the style of hat that the late Donny Hathaway use to wear, the father of R&B singer, Lalah Hathaway for you millennials. I didn't have a license, no defeating thoughts and no fear. All I had was my hunger, my determination and clear focus so I could get us to our destination. Even as a teenager, I knew I had abilities to someday achieve the goals and dreams that I held in my mind and in my heart. Up until we reached the border, it was a good idea. We arrived in Virginia and my mother found out that I drove the van most of the way there. She was not the happy mother that I spoke to the day before. Needless to say, I did not drive the van back to New Jersey.

My high school friend Chucky had become one of the guitar players for Millie Jackson and had the amazing opportunity to travel all over the country performing in major concert venues. By this time, I was not playing with any bands, I was just practicing a few times a week on my own. When Millie was performing in New Jersey or in New York, I would attend her shows with Chucky. There were a few times I would drive him up to Teaneck, New Jersey to meet the tour bus headed out on a concert tour.

One evening while on tour in California, Chucky called to ask me if I could do a show with them the following weekend in South Carolina. I immediately agreed, asking him to give me list of songs to learn. He told me which album the songs were on, so I went to the store to purchase the album so that I could learn the songs. The following week he and I rode up to Teaneck to get on the tour bus and head to South Carolina.

At the time I was still working so I took that Friday off to make the trip to perform at the show. When the weekend shows were finished, we'd get back on the bus heading back to New Jersey. The tour bus drivers were instructed to get me back in time so that I could go to work on Monday morning.

The following week I went back to work, which was a totally different lifestyle from being out on the road performing in different cities and states. Even though I was at work in a warehouse production environment, I was still experiencing the big 'stage show' feeling I felt while out on the road. There were other shows that I performed with Millie Jackson and the band occurring regularly. I had the opportunity to become the full-time bass guitarist for Millie Jackson.

About a month or so later, I was at home one evening and my phone rang, this time it wasn't Chucky, it was Millie Jackson on the other end. The fact that she called me herself let me know it was decision time. She was direct and straight to the point, as always. She said, "Skip, the other bass guitar player is not coming back to the band, and we are scheduled to go to England in a few weeks. We will be in England for three weeks and there are more shows scheduled in other countries following the England shows. The total estimated time for the tour will be approximately four months, non-stop, are you available?"

I froze in time for a few minutes because I did not have an answer. She needed an answer right on the spot. Lying on the bed next to where I was sitting, was Little Skip, my six-month old son. I had not too long ago gotten married, had a good paying job with benefits. With a new baby, I did not have an answer. I was in my mid-twenties and lacked life experience. I asked Millie what I should do. In retrospect, I know that Millie was not the person to ask that question. Of course, she told me that I had to make that decision on my own and to give her a call back in two days with an answer.

My final thought was, if I go to England, I will have to quit my good paying job, which was one of the world's largest beverage companies. I thought about my situation all day at work and even more the following day because that evening I had to call Millie with my answer. The more I thought about it, the sadder I began to feel, because by the time I left work that afternoon, I knew my answer.

Even though it has been many years since I had to make that phone call to Millie, while writing this paragraph I feel just a little of the emotion that I felt back then, because back during that time it caused me to go to a dark place in my life.

The next day I called Millie to let her know that I was not going to England with her and the band. She said that she understood and wished me well. With that being said, I knew it was the end of my performances with her and the group because she had to find another bass guitarist to take my place permanently. I recall lying on my bed after the phone call with Millie feeling the sadness. I just laid there for more than an hour looking at the ceiling thinking about the fact that I wasn't going to England with them.

After a while, I got up off the bed, got in my car and went for a long ride. As I was driving, I began to feel angry with myself because I was not in the position to go with them. While driving, I smoked a couple of joints of marijuana and a joint of boat a.k.a angel dust because I did not want to feel the sadness, anger and hurt I was feeling.

I drove for a while getting high and returned home really late. From being so high, I don't remember what time it was I returned, and I really don't remember driving back home. All I knew was I didn't want to feel anything, and I didn't want to face my situation. As days and weeks would go by, I was starting to get high more often, because by then the self-pity was starting to set in and join the other parties, sadness and inner anger parties.

Along with the marijuana and angel dust, I was beginning to use cocaine more often. Even though I wasn't using cocaine much in the past at that point, I needed more numbness. I was starting to use cocaine so regularly I figured if I buy more, I could sell some of it; make some money so that I could buy more for myself. I would buy an eight ball of cocaine, cut it and sell some, and I would still have enough for my own use. I wasn't considered a cocaine dealer, and if so, I was my own best customer. I was killing the pain, and I was beginning to take my life into a dark place.

By this time, my drug addiction was getting so out of control that it was beginning to affect a lot of areas of my life. I was getting high in some very unclean places, and could be found in some situations and environments I knew I should not have been in. I knew that I should not have been in those places, but at the time, all I was concerned with was taking that next hit of crack cocaine.

It was getting to the point where I was spending all the money I had just to get that hit and that feeling. Along with spending my paycheck money, I would also spend all the money I was earning, from playing in the band I was with at the time. The band was called Cheers, which was a predominantly Caucasian band except for me and the lead singer, who was an African American female. We performed at a lot of upscale events which paid us well, so the monies I was earning from Cheers band was also used to buy drugs.

At the time I joined the band, they had no idea that I had a drug addiction problem. Each time we had rehearsal or a gig I would keep my secret well disguised so that they would not notice my issue. Most of the band members were beer and alcohol drinkers, but they kept their drinking to a minimum because they were corporate workers and couldn't risk their main source of income.

As time went on, I began to be late for rehearsals and late for a few gigs, getting there in just enough time to plug up my bass guitar and start playing the first song. At one event, I smoked some cocaine before going to the gig. It was the reason I was late arriving. I made up some excuse that was convincing and there was nothing said about my tardiness. When the band took a break, I went into the restroom to finish the cocaine I had left over from earlier.

Again, I crushed the crack cocaine up and put it in my cigarette to smoke it. When we finished the gig, I took my money and headed back to the location that I was at earlier so that I could buy some more crack cocaine.

During a party gig in Princeton, New Jersey, the band was at the gig waiting for me to arrive. On this summer night I did not show up to the gig. I was at one of my regular locations getting high. I never called to let them know I wasn't coming to the gig. I thought about it, but I didn't go. I called them the next day to give them another excuse, but by then they were noticing a change in me and knew that I was lying. I could hear one of the other members in the background saying, "Fire him! He's a derelict and he's going to leave us hanging again!" I managed to convince them it would never happen again, that I was going to seek help.

I remained in the band and continued to perform other gigs with the Cheers band. I managed to disguise my drug use once again from the band to remain as a member. If they were to put me out of the band, I wouldn't have any other local bands to be a part of. All the bands in the area were filled with musicians. In 1992 during income tax return season, the s--t hit the fan. I was near rock bottom, and I knew it, and to think in the beginning of it all, I was only trying to put a bandage on the hurt that I was feeling due to not going to England with Millie Jackson and the band. The spiral continued.

The next day, I received my income tax check in the mail, and I was planning to cash it the next day. I felt that it was cause for a get high celebration. I already had money on me because I just got paid from my job, so I bought crack cocaine to get high. It was around 5pm in the evening when I started and went on for approximately four hours until I ran out of money.

I had already spent nearly two hundred dollars on crack cocaine, and I still wanted more. I didn't care about how I felt or how I looked, I wanted more cocaine. I went back to the lady I was buying the crack cocaine from and told her that I wanted some more but didn't have any money. I asked Lady J if she could give me some cocaine until the next day when I cashed my income tax check. She said she couldn't do it, so I asked her if she could cash my income tax check. She said that if I signed it and gave it to her, I could get more. I really didn't give a damn, so I signed my $600 income tax check and gave it to her. Lady J gave me a rock of crack cocaine which lasted me two hours. When I returned to her house, it was around 11:30pm and she gave me another rock of cocaine which lasted another two hours or so.

By the third rotation, I felt that I still credit from the balance. It was 1:30am and she was not answering her door. It had been over six hours that I had been getting high. After a few minutes she answered the door and said that she only had a little piece left. She gave me a much smaller piece of rock cocaine and told me not to come back. It was late and she said she didn't have any more. I told her that I would be back tomorrow evening to get my last piece of cocaine. I went back to the location that I was getting high at to smoke the last that I had. It was 3am Friday morning and I had been out almost ten hours getting high. I was high, smelly, and beginning to feel ashamed of myself for what I was doing to myself.

During this time, I wasn't living at home so after getting high for hours, I went to my mother's house to get some sleep. No one occupied the third-floor bedroom where my brother Sylvester and I slept during our middle school and teen years. I went to the third-floor bedroom to crash. When I made it upstairs, my mother opened the door and said that I needed to take a shower because I smelled. I managed to fall asleep for a few hours and woke up thinking about the last piece of cocaine that Lady J owed me.

It was Friday evening when I went back to her house to get my last rock that she owed me. When I went back, I had on my tuxedo for a gig later with the Cheers band. I smoked what I got from her and still wanted more. It was close to the time that I should have been heading to the gig to perform with Cheers band. I never went to the gig. I went to the Donnelly Homes Projects where I'd purchased drugs from before. I knew that it was possible to sell some items or trade for crack cocaine.

Wearing my tuxedo for the gig, the first thing I sold was a pair of sunglasses worth one hundred and fifty dollars. I think I got $25 for them. The next thing I sold was my watch for $25, along with a pair of binoculars for $20. Yes, binoculars. They are useful to drug dealers for looking out for the police. I was sitting on the floor of someone's apartment in a tuxedo smoking crack cocaine. Believe it not, I was well aware of what I was doing and by then I was beginning to hope that someone would come and rescue me.

There was nothing else to sell except my bass guitar, which was in the trunk of my grandmother's car I was driving at the time. As I sat there on the floor getting high, I remember someone saying I didn't have to sit on the floor. The reason that I was sitting on the floor was because I was in someone's bedroom. I don't know whose room it was, but I know that I did not want to sit on a stranger's bed. I was high, I wasn't dumb. It was bad enough that I was in a stranger's home. I didn't know what had been on that bed.

That day when I was nearly finished smoking all the cocaine, I knew I was coming to the end of my crack cocaine addiction. I knew because as I smoked that last bit of it, I was losing the desire and urge to get more. Somehow, I was beginning to feel a sense of peace, serenity and clarity come over me. There were no jitters, no paranoia, no urge, no desire, no guilt, and no shame.

I got up off the floor, brushed off my clothes, put on my trench coat and told the individuals there that I had to leave. As I left the Donnelly Homes apartments and drove my grandmother's car to my mother's house, I knew that I did not want to get high anymore.

I parked the car in the driveway, went into the house, and immediately went upstairs to the third-floor bedroom. I took off my trench coat, sat on the bed, and asked God to take the addiction out of my life because I didn't want to get high anymore. That night my prayers were answered, because for the past thirty years I have not touched crack cocaine, other drugs, nor had the desire to do so. For many years I prayed that I would release all my past life challenges and issues, and one day become the confident and secure person that I always wanted to become.

God helped me to understand that no matter what my past may have been, I could begin to create the life and lifestyle that I truly desired. I came to realize and understand that by me not continuing to remain the bass guitarist for Millie Jackson wasn't the root cause of my drug addiction, I realized that my childhood bedwetting issues was also a major part of my addiction. I came to understand that I was covering my past childhood issues even at a young age and didn't realize that I was doing so. From dating unlimited girls in junior high school into high school, and continuing the same dating cycle into adulthood, I was covering up the shame and lack of confidence that I felt about myself for many years. Now, the shame, doubt and lack of confidence is gone, I have come out of the fire.

I am now using the darkness of my past - life experiences to help other people who may be going through and experiencing challenges and issues, to understand that they have the power to change and overcome almost any of their own life's experiences. Sometimes you may have to go through the fire, but you don't have to sit and remain in it. It's time to take the next step and come through the fire.

If a little country boy who once picked potatoes and tomatoes in the hot field in Cape Charles, Va. and later on in life became addicted to drugs as an adult, overcame it and Walked Through The Fire, so can you...

You have come to the end of this book anthology entitled Through the Fire Stories of Strength, Courage and Resilience. I hope that you were able to glean something from each one of the 14 contributors that would help you in some area or aspect of your life. Just know that no matter what you have been through, are going through or will go through God is with you every step of the way. It my hope that you were able to see woven throughout each of our stories is that our faith kept us in the midst of the fire and it helped us to come through the fire.

As a coach and counselor it my goal to help people heal from the hurt and trauma of their past so that they can become the men and women that God has called each one of to be. Our paths and our stories are all different, but we didn't allow that to keep us stuck. What we did was turn the pain into purpose. We all recognized that we are stronger than our struggles. I hope that you can recognize that you too have purpose and that you are stronger than you think. You too can come Through the Fire.

Gwen Goolsby-Tillery is a Minister, speaker, coach, counselor and entrepreneur that is passionate about helping Kingdom people reach their full potential so they can experience the success that God has promised so that they walk in their purpose. For more information regarding her programs, coaching, training, and books or for speaking engagements please visit www.successarize.com

Made in the USA
Monee, IL
02 June 2022

14f0d6b1-21fb-441d-bf8d-1f8b56329af7R01